Texas Fish & Game®

presents

TEXAS Waterfowl

by Chester Moore

OTHER TITLES PUBLISHED BY
TEXAS FISH & GAME PUBLISHING CO., LLC

BOOKS:

THE Texas Deer Book
by Steve LaMascus & Greg Rodriguez

Saltwater Strategies®: Flounder Fever
by Chester Moore, Jr.

Saltwater Strategies®: Where, When & How to Wadefish Texas
by Bink Grimes

**Freshwater Strategies®: A Practical Approach
to Texas Freshwater Fishing**
by Doug Pike

Saltwater Strategies®: Texas Reds
by Chester Moore, Jr.

Saltwater Strategies®: Texas Trout Tactics
by Chester Moore, Jr.

**Saltwater Strategies®: Pat Murray's No-Nonsense
Guide to Coastal Fishing**
by Pat Murray

Texas Saltwater Classics: Fly Patterns for the Texas Coast
by Greg Berlocher

Doreen's 24 Hour Eat Gas Now Café
by Reavis Z. Wortham

PERIODICALS:

Texas Fish & Game Magazine (12x/year)
Texas Lakes & Bays Atlas (annual)

for information, contact us at:
1-800-750-4678
www.fishgame.com
Texas Fish & Game Publishing Co., LLC
1745 Greens Road • Houston, Texas 77032

Texas Fish & Game®

presents

TEXAS
Waterfowl

by Chester Moore

TEXAS FISH & GAME
PUBLISHING CO., L.L.C.

1745 Greens Road • Houston, Texas 77032
1-800-750-4678
www.fishgame.com

Published by

TEXAS FISH & GAME
PUBLISHING CO., L.L.C.

1745 Greens Road
Houston Texas 77032
Phone: 281-227-3001 Fax: 281-227-3002
Website: www.fishgame.com

First Edition

Foreword by Nick Gilmore

All photos by Chester Moore unless otherwise credited.

Design and production by Wendy Kipfmiller

Edited by Don Zaidle.

ISBN: 0-929980-04-2

To God, for his amazing creation, and for blessing hunters with our true best friend—the dog. Without them, we would not have nearly as much fun out there.

Contents

foreword

It isn't difficult to pick out the waterfowlers in a group of Texas hunters these days. They are the ones with the big smiles on their faces.

But it wasn't always so. Back in the 1980s and into the early 90s, our ducks were going through some hard times. As duck numbers dropped, bag limits tightened. Hunters, except for the truly dedicated die-hards, were hanging up their decoys, casing their shotguns, and putting away their waders. Depending on where in the state they lived, the point system limited many of them to a brief season at best with very little shooting. The right kinds of ducks just were not there, and a misplaced shot or misidentified species could turn a pleasant outing into a one-shot hunt. Too much of that kind of hunting forced many a good retriever into early gun-dog retirement.

Fortunately, the picture for goose hunters was not so dim. Indeed, many a duck man had turned to geese for his waterfowling pleasure. With high goose numbers being recorded, the biggest fear was that hunters couldn't shoot enough birds to keep their numbers in check. It was highly touted among waterfowl biologists that all the great goose shooting could come to a screeching halt if ordinary diseases started spreading like an epidemic through the overpopulated flocks.

But that was then and this is now. Except for a few species, duck populations are being recorded in numbers not seen in a recent lifetime. The goose populations we feared would be wiped out are now higher than ever, and we currently fear they may eat themselves out of house and home.

Texas waterfowling has never been better. New generations of duck and goose hunters are heading to the fields and marshes every season, and many an old hand is returning to the sport he loves. Good times have returned and they should be enjoyed for as long as they last.

And that's exactly why Chester Moore has written this book.

There are two reasons for a book to exist. One is for entertainment and the other is to pass on knowledge. If you are neither entertained nor educated by what you find in this book, then the fault surely will not lie with its author. Chester is a waterfowler and he knows what he's writing about.

I have known Chester both personally and professionally for more than a decade. He is a talented and dependable writer on almost any subject he cares to tackle, and I know he cares about the future of hunting and fishing in Texas. A longtime waterfowler, Chester is as much at home in a goose blind or on a duck marsh as he is at his computer keyboard. Being a good hunter and a good writer is a rare combination these days. I am sure you will realize the value of that combination as you work your way through these pages.

If what Chester has penned here helps you to better understand the world of Texas waterfowl, and in the process puts more enjoyment in your trips to the field, then he will have accomplished his goal in writing on this subject that's so close to his heart.

Here's hoping that you make the most of your waterfowling opportunities this fall, and for many hunting seasons to come. —Nick Gilmore, Editor, *Texas Sportsman* magazine

Introduction

The familiar sound of whistling wings sounded overhead in the predawn darkness, followed by a series of "splooshes." The sounds hinted at the soul-stirring action to come as a swollen, orange sun peeked over the horizon.

A million thoughts raced through my head as I wondered exactly what ducks were landing in the decoys. Were they the fast-flying greenwinged teal I had seen while scouting the area the day before? Maybe they were widgeon, ringneck—or pintail!

Intrigue hung thick in the air.

As the sun's brilliance steadily vanquished the darkness, my father and I could make out a few greenwings on the outer edge of the decoys, teasing me as shooting time was still a full five minutes away. I figured they would leave before we could legally click off our safeties and be on our way to some prime gumbo ingredients, but I really did not care. Just being in their presence was enough for me. Even in dim light, their beauty was radiant.

Almost as if they had read my mind, the cluster of teal rose off the water a minute before they would have met a barrage of steel shot, but I knew there would be more action to come. I could feel it.

As the clock struck 6:53, I blew on my call and we readied our guns—the game was officially on. High in the sky, I spotted four gadwall giving the spread a look-over. As I let out a couple of quacks, the quartet dived from the heavens straight toward the decoys. I clicked my safety off as my heart pounded in anticipation. The ducks continued their descent, and a few yards before slamming headfirst into the water, they put on the brakes, turned into a landing position with wings cupped and legs out, and Dad and I unloaded on them.

All four ducks fell, and we were off to an absolutely perfect morning of duck hunting off a remote creek in Newton County, Texas.

My friends know that besides coastal fishing, duck and goose hunting is tops in my book. In fact, from November through January, I am obsessed with it. Occasionally, someone will ask how I could be so fired up over getting up at a ridiculously early hour, lugging dozens of decoys through knee-deep mud, and tangling with mosquitoes, snakes, and alligators—and that is just in the early teal season in Texas!

In California, I have walked through 3 feet of snow half a mile across a field near the base of Mount Shasta to hunt Canada geese in 7-degree temperatures. In New York, I have faced chilling sub-zero winds off Lake Ontario to bag mallard and merganser, been ravaged by deer flies in the early resident Canada goose season; and nearly got frostbite hunting divers on Owasco Lake.

In my home state of Texas (and my frequent destination of Louisiana), I have logged hundreds of hunts over the years in every kind of conditions imaginable, in the process pulling hamstrings while walking through gumbo mud, pulling my back out pushing my boat off of a tidal flat, and generally wearing myself to a nub by season's end.

Why would an otherwise sane person do such things to himself? It is all about the birds.

The beauty, mystery, and intensity embodied in ducks and geese have captivated me since I was a youngster jumping wood duck on creek beds in Jasper County. God reserved the finest strokes of his paintbrush of creation for the waterfowl of the world. Just look at a wood duck. Can you think of anything that we pursue as hunters more beautiful than that? Yes, whitetail deer are gorgeous, as are elk and just about every other game animal out there. I truly love them all, but in the looks department, woodies, pintail, widgeon, and teal put them all to shame.

Then there is the matter of flight. Anyone that has seen mallard navigate timber, or a big pintail drake ride the wind currents over a coastal marsh, has seen true magic in action. Deer might be smarter, but I would like to see one drop out of the sky from 100 yards and land gracefully.

Another part of this great quest is the camaraderie. In duck blinds, you can talk, joke, eat, and do all kinds of stuff forbidden in other outdoors pursuits. I laugh and smile more while duck hunting than when doing anything else that involves guns.

Maybe best of all are the dogs. The various retrievers are the most loyal, hard-working, and amazing dogs on the planet. They are always happy to hunt. My dad's friend, the late Harold Staggs, had a dog that would throw decoys at the house at night when it heard geese flying over. That is dedication.

For me, it is a natural extension of my deep love for coastal fishing. In fact, it was while fishing as a kid that I first was hooked on ducks. Routinely seeing pintail, mottled duck, and scaup while fishing for reds, specks, and flounder hooked me into this whole waterfowl-hunting thing. One of the greatest things in the world is going duck hunting in the morning and catching redfish and trout in the afternoon. Outfitters and outdoor writers call this "cast and blast." I call it "heaven on Earth."

To those on the outside, that might seem a bit strange, but I have a feeling anyone that has picked up this book understands perfectly. They know that the pursuit of ducks and geese is something truly special, and like me, will do whatever it takes to be in the presence of waterfowl, preferably armed with a 12-gauge stoked with No. 4 shot, and in company with a good retriever.

Sounds like heaven on Earth to me.

Chapter One

The Life and Times of Waterfowl

A big part of my fascination with waterfowl is there are so many intriguing facets to their life history, biology, and conservation. Having studied a variety of species throughout my life, there are undoubtedly more "damn, that was cool" moments when investigating the intricacies of ducks and geese than with anything else we hunt or fish for in Texas.

Think about it for a second. How many times have you argued with your friends in the blind about which duck species in the fastest, or pondered just how quickly those specklebelly migrated down from Canada? The trait of intercontinental migration alone makes waterfowl unique among the species we hunt, and when you factor in the biological diversity among species, things get interesting, as you will read in the following text.

THE DUCK LIFE CYCLE

Just as I was preparing to write this book, Ducks Unlimited provided me with a great breakdown of the life cycle of ducks:

- **Pre-nesting:** The female duck always makes the choice for the breeding area because she is homing to the site of her birth, or to a site where she successfully hatched a nest.

- **Nesting:** If you were a predator searching several square miles for a meal, encountering a duck nest would seem like a long shot. However, suppose that the nests are concentrated in small patches and in thin strips of grass. Suddenly, your odds are looking up. Although intuitive, the relationship between nest success and grassland expanse was only recently confirmed by U.S. Fish and Wildlife Service biologists while evaluating the benefits of Conservation Reserve Program (CRP) to ducks.

- **Brood Rearing:** The more time a hen spends taking care of young ducklings, the less time she has to take care of herself. This precious balance must be met to maximize both the hens' and ducklings' chances of survival. To keep ducklings healthy, a hen must brood or keep ducklings warm until they can do it themselves, help ducklings find a good source of food, ensure family bonding as a unit, guide young ducks during migration, and help them locate staging and wintering habitat. The most important time in a duckling's life is the first two weeks. This is when the hen must put forth the most energy to keep her ducklings together and safe. A hen's chance of death increases when she is defending her ducklings.

- **Post-Breeding:** This is the period in the annual life cycle of a duck backed by breeding and nesting. Mallards are required to find energy sources to fuel the activities of raising a brood, keeping them healthy and re-growing feathers during molt. These energy-expending activities take place during the post-breeding period. Scientists speculate that the reason for drake (male) mallards outnumbering hens in the population is the result of higher death rate among hens during the post-breeding period. During the post-breeding period, ducks can experience nutritional stress.

PHOTO COURTESY OF THE U.S. FISH AND WILDLIFE SERVICE

A gadwall hen and her young swim on a pond in the prairie pothole region. Predation during this time can be great from a variety of creatures, ranging from red foxes to raccoons and hawks.

Nutritional stress is where nutrients demanded by the body exceed the amount of nutrients a duck is able to find and eat.

• **Molting:** Ducks depend on their feathers, and old, worn feathers must be replaced. Molting is the process of replacing worn feathers. Ducks molt in late summer and early spring. During the fall, ducks molt synchronously, or lose and replace all of their feathers in a short period. Synchronous molting renders ducks flightless during a portion of this time, thus at greater risk from predators until the new feathers come in. Losing and replacing all feathers can take up to two weeks. The new feathers are drab in color and considered a duck's basic plumage. In the early spring, just as the breeding season gets underway, a partial loss of feathers happens when the male ducks put on their alternate plumage. Feathers are largely made up of proteins, and account for almost one-third of all protein in the body. The need for large quantities of high protein

3

food might be one reason that male ducks and unsuccessful nesting hens leave the breeding grounds for special molting grounds far away, thereby reducing competition for limited protein resources.

- **Fall Migration:** Birds migrate long distances from wintering grounds to breeding areas, and back again to the wintering grounds using visual and nonvisual navigation clues. Visual orientation mechanisms include the sun, polarized light, stars, and landmarks. Birds use the axes of polarized light to determine the position of the sun and perform sun compass orientation. Navigation at night requires using stars. Experiments performed in planetariums have shown that some birds actually use a stellar map to find their way around at night. Landmarks might be important for navigation—not as compasses, but as directional clues. Coastlines, mountain ridges, and waterways such as the Mississippi River are major topographic features that might be considered landmarks. One nonvisual cue that aids in navigation is the Earth's magnetic field. When the Earth's magnetic field is obstructed, migrating birds often change or alternate direction and altitude. Homing, another nonvisual clue, is a bird's ability to find its way home when released in an unfamiliar place or direction. The ability to navigate over many miles from breeding to wintering grounds is an amazing adaptation. It is likely that most birds use a combination of visual and nonvisual cues, as well as homing. Navigation and migration behavior is very difficult to study therefore has not been fully resolved.

- **Wintering:** Everyone knows that ducks fly south in the winter, but what do they do when they get there, and where do they do it? Ducks spend much of their time in the southern portions of the United States and along the coastal fringes, where weather conditions are mild. They leave northern nesting areas and head for a warmer climate for several reasons, least of which is because the weather is cold. During much of the winter, ducks loaf about eating and storing up nutrients in preparation for the long trip back to the breeding grounds. Waterfowl can withstand very cold temperatures, but when their food source is eliminated, they must leave northern areas in search of mild temperatures. When shallow ponds or lakes freeze over, ducks can no longer reach aquatic plants and insects for meals. Ducks that feed on seeds or waste grain must also leave the area when snow covers their foods. Ducks winter in mild areas where food is plentiful and the water rarely freezes, such as the Mississippi Alluvial Valley in the southern United States. Other optimal wintering place for ducks include coastal northern California and along the central valley of California.

FACTS & FIGURES

An article in *Southeastern Naturalist* reported on a study by Ruth M. Elsey, Phillip L. Trosclair III, and Jeb T. Linscombe on the predation of mottled ducks by alligators:

"Although the alligator has been noted to prey upon mottled ducks, evidence of mottled duck consumption is rare in numerous studies of alligator food habits. This might be due to the season and habitat from which alligators were collected for evaluation (often autumn samples from deep water habitats preferred by adult alligators). We examined stomach contents of alligators in summer (when mottled duck broods and molting adults are flightless) from shallow water habitats preferred by mottled ducks. Mottled duck remains were found in 20.9 percent of 43 alligator stomachs examined, far more than the highest frequency occurrence previously reported (1.27 percent). Unexpectedly, three relatively small alligators (1.51-1.70 m total length) consumed mottled ducks and the sixteen largest alligators did not. This study underscores the importance of season and location of collections when evaluating stomach content data."

The big white ducks, commonly kept as pets and fixtures in many city parks, are Peking ducks brought over from China in the 1870s for meat production. Muscovy, which hail from South America, are also popular meat ducks, and feral specimens sometimes hybridize with mallards and mottled ducks.

PHOTO COURTESY OF THE U.S. FISH AND WILDLIFE SERVICE

The red-breasted merganser has been clocked flying as fast as 80 miles per hour

- Ducks Unlimited charted band return data from 1990 to 2000 for all duck species banded north of Texas during the breeding season, and then identified the top five duck production areas for the state. Of the 5403 duck bands reported in Texas, 37 percent were banded in Saskatchewan, 19 percent in Alberta, 6 percent in Manitoba, 5 percent in North Dakota, and 5 percent in Montana. Mallard represented the majority (41 percent) of banded birds harvested in Texas. Blue-winged teal (16 percent), wood duck (12 percent), and pintail (10 percent) were the next closest species.

DU noted it quickly becomes apparent how important mallard, blue-winged teal, and wood duck are to Texas hunters when over 69 percent of band recoveries come from these three species.

Also according to DU, just about every county in Texas produced at least one band recovery, but counties located along the Texas coast reported the most. The top five counties were Jefferson, Fort Bend, Wharton, Calhoun, and Chambers in that order.

- Duck eggshells have tiny holes (pores) that allow it to breathe. According to the Provincial Museum of Alberta, eggs can have 7500 pores, most found at the blunt end of the egg. Respiratory gasses as well as water vapor travel through these pores, allowing the egg to breathe."
- A popular urban legend concerning ducks is that a duck's quack doesn't echo. This is not true, and a team from the University of Salford in England proved it with a research project.
- The lifespan of a mallard is typically two to three years, although wild specimens have been found living longer than 10 years, and one domestic mallard hung around until it was 27.
- An adult Canada goose can eat up to 4 pounds of grass in one day. Imagine the damage a flock of 1000 can do to a field.
- According to the popular facts and figures website, planet101.com, the fastest waterfowl species in flight is the Asian spur-winged goose, which has been clocked at 88 miles per hour. The red-breasted merganser is a close second at 80 mile per hour. The canvasback, although one of the largest ducks, can hit an amazing 72 miles per hour. Eider are good for up to 70 miles an hour, while teal can hit 68. Mallard and pintail are tied at 65 mile per hour. I was able to independently verify the speeds for most of these species and found that when these birds are flying high, tailwinds

Canada geese are becoming increasingly problematic as their numbers increase. They nest on golf courses in many parts of the country, and have even been known to attack golfers.

can push them to even more amazing speeds. The red-breasted merganser, for example, was clocked by researches flying 100 miles per hour with the help of tailwinds.

- Baby ducks are born precocial—not fully dependent on their parents for food, have both eyes open, and sport a warm coat of down. The young of other birds such as songbirds are born altricial—naked, blind, and fully dependent on parents for food and warmth.

- According to research conducted by Michael R. Miller, John Y. Takekawa, Joseph P. Fleskes, Dennis L. Orthmyer, David A. Haukos, and William M. Perry, pintail migrate with an average groundspeed of 77 kilometers (47.8 miles) per hour, which is within the range of estimates reported in literature for migratory and local flights of waterfowl. The ground speed averaged 53 kilometers (32.9 miles) per hour in headwinds and 82 kilometers (50.9 miles) per hour in tailwinds.

- Canada geese can live up to 24 years and mate for life. If their mate is lost, they will usually find another mate, but some research suggests some geese never do.

- Cornell researchers report that one snow goose nest was attended by two females but no male. What they found was that each female had been impregnated by a different male and both of them incubated the eggs.

- Cornell researchers conducted studies on snow goose genetics. What they found about the dark color of the blue morph is fascinating: If a pure dark goose mates with a white goose, the offspring will all be dark (possibly with white bellies). If two white geese mate, they have only white off-spring. If two dark geese mate, they will have mostly dark offspring, but might have a few white ones, too.

- Swans can live up to 35 years in captivity, and mate for life. On the East Coast, swans are hunted by permit. Some specimens get as large as 25 pounds with a 5-foot wingspan.

- Ducks are born with no blood vessels or nerves in their feet, so they cannot feel cold water.

The flight speed of ducks is hotly debated, and most hunters would be surprised to see the real data.

- In the late nineteenth century and early twentieth century, the canvasback was heavily hunted commercially. This eventually led to the population being brought down to dangerous levels.

- Ducks and geese have killed lots of people. Well, not intentionally. The airline industry estimates 350 people have died in accidents precipitated by bird-airplane collisions. A CNN report shows that Canada geese are the primary culprits in bird-plane collisions. Goose populations have quadrupled to 2 million since 1985. The airline industry is keeping up, with 28 million jet takeoffs and landings in the U.S. alone, compared to 18 million in 1980.

Snow goose numbers have skyrocketed to the point of being a danger to themselves. Hunter harvest using electronic calls has helped keep the population in balance.

"I think the public should definitely be aware that birds and other wildlife can cause hazards at airports, and they need to be supportive of efforts that airports are making to minimize these problems," said Richard Dolbeer, Bird Strike Committee USA chairperson. Between 1990 and 1998, birds and planes collided more than 22,000 times in the United States. Most of these strikes were routine, but some weren't."

According to the CNN report, in 1995, an Air Force radar plane crashed in Alaska, killing 24 crewmen, after geese were sucked into one of the plane's engines.

- Before the era of modern sport hunting was born in the early 1900s, wood duck were hunted almost to extinction. Wise hunters and others interested in conservation helped to bring the numbers back by putting out nest boxes. The result has been the wood duck is now the most common duck in the Atlantic Flyway, and one of the most common throughout Texas and in the Mississippi Flyway.

- The black-bellied whistling duck does not quack; it lets out a high whistling noise that is sometimes described as "descending."

- Gadwall populations saw a huge increase in the 1990s into the 2000s, but the last couple of years saw a slight decrease in their numbers. Scientists are not sure what is going on with the species, but hunters are generally happy to be killing lots of them in Texas.

- The Florida Museum of Natural History notes that alligator garfish have been reported to attack duck decoys and eat injured waterfowl shot by hunters.

- Waterfowl sometimes end up in strange places. Brian Fischer of Drake Plantation Outfitters shot a Pacific brant on the prairie near Winnie, Texas. Brant are unheard of in Texas.

- The rare long-tailed duck is serious about diving. They have been recorded to dive as deep as 180 feet in search of mussels and clams. Compared to an emperor penguin, that is minor league; they have been recorded as deep as 1,584 feet off the coast of Antarctica.

ABOUT DUCK STAMPS

Ducks Stamps are the beautifully detailed stamps that the U.S. Postal Service produces for the U.S. Fish and Wildlife Service (USFWS) to raise funds for wetlands conservation. They were first created in 1934 as the federal license required for hunting any kind of migratory waterfowl, but their benefits stretch far beyond the realms of law enforcement.

According to USFWS, since 1934 the sale of Federal Duck Stamps has generated more than $670 million, which has been used to help purchase or lease over 5.2 million acres of waterfowl habitat in the U.S. These lands are now protected in the National Wildlife Refuge System.

Waterfowl are not the only wildlife to benefit from the sale of Federal Duck Stamps. Numerous other bird, mammal, fish, reptile, and amphibian species that rely on wetland habitats have prospered. Further, an estimated one-third of the nation's endangered and threatened species find food or shelter in refuges established using Federal Duck Stamp funds.

PHOTO COURTESY OF USFWS

The 2002 Federal Duck Stamp featured a wood duck. The image changes every year and is chosen from among sub-missions by artists from around the country

People, too, have benefited from the Federal Duck Stamp Program. Hunters have places to enjoy their hunting heritage, and other outdoor enthusiasts have places to hike, watch birds, and visit. Moreover, the protected wetlands help purify water supplies, store flood-water, reduce soil erosion and sedimentation, and provide spawning areas for fish important to sport and commercial fishermen.

USFWS officials said that 98 cents out of every dollar generated by duck stamp sales goes directly to purchase land for the national wildlife refuge system.

Chapter Two

Waterfowl Identification

Waterfowl identification is an art, and like any art form, it is one you have to learn in the field by viewing birds in flight, on the water, and during different parts of the season. In other words, it takes time.

This chapter is designed to give you a head start learning to identify ducks and geese, and for those who are already experts, it gives useful information about range, habits, and the quirks that make them so darn fascinating.

Are you sure that mallard hen you shot was really a mallard? Maybe it was a mottled or shoveler? What about that strange looking ruddy duck your friend shot a few years ago? Was it really a ruddy, or could it have been the mysterious Mexican masked duck?

For visual clues to give a better idea of what these ducks look like, see the color Waterfowl Identification section beginning on page C/1.

Read on and you will see that everything in the world of waterfowl is not always what it seems.

WATERFOWL PROFILES

Species: Lesser Scaup *(see page C/14)*

Nicknames: bluebill

Range: These divers nest from the west-central United States into the northern tip of the Yukon Territories.

In Texas: Scaup love big water and gang up in huge concentrations on the larger reservoirs like Toledo Bend, and along the Texas estuaries from Sabine Lake to Corpus Christi Bay.

Description: Mature males have a black head that has a purple or green sheen. They have a peaked head with a bright, yellow eye and bluish-gray bill. The backs are gray with white/gray flanks, and a black under tail. Hens have a brown head, back, and breast. Many times, they have a white patch at the base of the beak.

Calls: Females produce a low growling type noise. Males make a "whee-o" sound.

Similar to: Ring-necked duck and greater scaup

Interesting facts: Scaup populations have plummeted in recent years, and scientists are not sure why. They are voracious predators of fresh-water shrimp, and in the prairie breeding ground areas, there seems to be a decline in these crustaceans. Ducks Unlimited scientists believe this could be part of the problem.

Species: Greater Scaup *(see page C/1)*

Nicknames: bluebill

Range: These divers nest in the extreme northern tundra areas from Hudson Bay throughout Alaska into Siberia.

In Texas: Most greater scaup in Texas winter along the Central and South Texas coast on the bays from Rockport to Lower Laguna Madre.

Description: Mature males have a black head that has a purple or green sheen. They have a peaked head with a bright, yellow eye and bluish-gray bill. The backs are gray with white/gray flanks and a black undertail. Hens have a brown head, back, and breast. Many times, they have a white patch at the base of the beak.

Calls: Females produce a low growling type noise. Males make a "whee-o" sound.

Similar to: Ring-necked duck and greater scaup

Interesting facts: It is extremely difficult to distinguish the greater and lesser scaup. They tend to be larger and look "fat" compared to the more streamlined lesser scaup.

Species: Northern Shoveler *(see page C/1)*

Nicknames: spoonbill, spoony, digger, shovelhead, Hollywood duck, smiling mallard

Range: Shoveler nest in the western tier of the prairie pothole region north through Alaska and the Yukon Territories. They winter throughout the southern United States.

In Texas: Hunters are likely to encounter them anywhere, as they have a penchant for freshwater and tidal marshes. The Upper Coast holds the largest numbers, particularly the flooded rice fields in Chambers and Jefferson counties.

Description: Both the male and female have a beak you will never forget. It is very shovel- or spoon-like, bulbous and broad at the tip. Mature males have a green head and neck with a conspicuous yellow eye and a large black beak. The breast is white and the flank is brown. The feet are orange. Immature males that hunters take early in the season have a lot of brown on the chest. Females have a mottled body with an orange beak that has black on top. The eyes are brown.

Calls: Females let out a low-pitched "quack."

Similar to: The mature drakes look a lot like a mallard drake.

Hens are very similar in appearance to many puddle ducks, including hen mallard, gadwall, black duck, and mottled.

Interesting facts: Hunters sometimes look down on shoveler because of their appearance and the habit of eating pretty much anything. When they are eating rice, they taste just fine and are indistinguishable from most other ducks.

Species: Bufflehead *(see page C/1)*

Nicknames: buffalo head

Range: These handsome ducks breed in Canada and Alaska, and winter throughout most of the United States into northern Mexico.

In Texas: Hunters can expect to encounter bufflehead in the bays on the Gulf Coast. The Aransas and Copano Bay complex tends to hold the largest concentrations.

Description: Bufflehead are the smallest diving duck in North America. Mature males have a black head that in soft light shows a rainbow-like iridescence. They have a large white patch extending from the eye around the head. They have a gray beak, white underbelly, black back, and pink legs; they are not very manly looking. Females are medium brown on the top and have a light brown underside. They have a gray beak, small white patch on the cheeks, and gray legs.

Calls: Females make a bizarre, short croaking sound.

Similar to: hooded merganser, common and Barrow's goldeneye

Interesting facts: They are so small they almost exclusively use the nest cavities of woodpeckers, especially the northern flicker. Bufflehead hens lay eggs more slowly than any duck, usually taking two to three days between eggs.

Species: Ring-Necked Duck *(see page C/2)*

Nicknames: ringbill, blackjack

Range: They nest throughout Canada and winter mainly in the southern half of the United States.

In Texas: These birds winter along the coast and in the backwaters of river systems.

Description: The breeding males are a bold mixture of black and white while the females are a dull brown and sport a white eye-ring. They are easy to tell apart from scaup by the ring around the bill, which is easier to see than the dull one around the necks.

Calls: Females make a low growling noise.

Similar to: lesser and greater scaup

Interesting facts: Ringnecks have an incredibly varied diet that allows them to feed in areas inhospitable to most ducks.

Species: Northern Mallard *(see page C/2)*

Nicknames: greenhead (drake), winter mallard

Range: Mallard nest throughout much of North America and into Canada, and many winter in the southern United States.

In Texas: The Pineywoods of East Texas is a good place to find mallard, as are the rivers and reservoirs in the Texas Panhandle region.

Description: Males have a brown chest, gray underside and back, green head, and yellow beak. Females are mottled brown and have a yellowish beak.

Calls: Females make a loud "quack" while males make a weird, "reebing" noise.

Similar to: black duck, mottled duck, gadwall, northern shoveler

Interesting facts: Mallard are the most common duck in the United States and receive the most hunting pressure. Despite this, hunters annually take only about 1 percent of the population.

Species: Mottled Duck *(see page C/14)*

Nicknames: black mallard, summer mallard

Range: Along the Gulf Coast and up the Atlantic Coast into Georgia

In Texas: The Gulf Coast from Port Arthur down to Port Aransas holds the most mottled.

Description: They are a mottled brown/black color.

Calls: Females make a loud quacking noise.

Similar to: black duck, mallard, northern shoveler, gadwall

Interesting facts: When Texas Parks & Wildlife Department officials do alligator stomach content checks, they often find mottled ducks inside.

Species: Pintail *(see page C/2)*

Nicknames: sprig, sprig duck, bull spring (drake)

Range: Pintails nest in Canada and Alaska, and winter in the southern half of the United States.

In Texas: Pintails can show up anywhere, but prefer the Gulf Coast.

Description: Males have a white breast and lower neck with a gray body, dark brown head, and grayish/blue bill. When mature, they have a large tail feather extending from the body, hence the name. Females are a mottled brown/black color and have a grayish/blue bill.

Calls: Females make a quack while males whistle. While feeding, they make a strange vibrating type sound.

Similar to: gadwall, female mallard, female northern shoveler

Interesting facts: Under the infamous point regulations system of the 1970s, hunters could kill 10 pintails. Now, populations of this magnificent bird have fallen dramatically due to habitat loss in the breeding grounds. Over the past few seasons, the pintail daily limit has been one drake, and is expected to remain so for the foreseeable future.

Species: Wood Duck *(see page C/3)*

Nicknames: woody

Range: Wood ducks are Texas residents that nest in tree cavities. They range from the Pacific Coast to the East coast.

In Texas: The Pineywoods of East Texas is the best place to find these beautiful ducks in the back woods and along creek drainages.

Description: The male has the most beautifully marked head of any duck, with a greenish/black pattern, white outlining, a red eye, and a red/white/yellow beak. Females have a dull brown/gray body with a white mask around the eyes.

Calls: The males are famous for their squeaky whistle.

Similar to: Hens are similar to female mergansers.

Interesting facts: One of the major predators of nests is rat snakes, which are excellent climbers and often steal the eggs. Raccoons are also significant predators. Snakes and raccoons sometimes kill brooding hens.

Species: Goldeneye *(see page C/3)*

Nicknames: James Bond duck (a reference to the Bond movie "Goldeneye")

Range: Goldeneye are a duck of the Pacific Northwest, both nesting and wintering there.

In Texas: A small number appear in Texas every year, and tend to hang out along the coast. Sabine Lake and the bays around Rockport probably harbor the most.

Description: They are a medium-sized diver with a fat body. Males have black and white all over, and the distinctive goldish-yellow eye. The head is black, but in good light, you can see a mallard green-like hue. Females are quite a bit smaller and gray with a brown head.

Calls: In courtship, males let out a "ca-ca" sound.

Similar to: bufflehead, hooded merganser

Interesting facts: Goldeneye can tolerate very cold temperatures. They are a staple in the Sierra Nevada mountain region during winter, as they have no problem dealing with ice and snow.

Species: Barrow's Goldeneye *(see page C/9)*

Nicknames: none

Range: Like the "common" goldeneye, these birds are most common in the Pacific Northwest, both nesting and wintering there.

In Texas: Very few of these ducks make it to Texas, but they inhabit the same areas as common goldeneye. I saw one while wade-fishing the Anahuac Refuge shoreline a few years ago.

Description: They are a medium-sized diver with a fat body. Males have black and white all over with the distinctive goldish-yellow eye, and a row of white spots along black wings. Common goldeneye do not have the spots. Females are quite a bit smaller, and gray with a brown head.

Calls: In courtship, males let out a "ca-ca" sound.

Similar to: bufflehead, hooded merganser

Interesting facts: The females are not particular about their nests, and often leave the young in the nests of other ducks like wood duck and bufflehead.

Species: Blue-Winged Teal *(see page C/3)*

Nicknames: bluewing

Range: They nest in the prairie pothole region of the United States into northern Canada, and winter from Texas to South America. I saw bluewing while fishing Venezuela's Lake Guri in December 1999.

In Texas: They prefer coastal marshes with widgeon grass present, and love rice fields.

Description: Bluewing are tiny ducks. Both the male and female are a dull brown with blue stripes on the wings. Males have a white, crescent-shaped pattern on the face and in the rear area. This develops as winter comes, and most males do not show this during the early teal season.

Calls: The females quack while the males let out high-pitched whistles.

Similar to: green-winged teal

Interesting facts: These are the first ducks to migrate south, and have their own early hunting season in Texas in September.

Species: Green-Winged Teal *(see page C/4)*

Nicknames: greenwing, common teal

Range: They nest in the prairie pothole region of the United States into northern Canada, and winter from Texas to Mexico.

In Texas: They prefer coastal marshes and love rice fields. They also show up in fair numbers on Sam Rayburn reservoir.

Description: These tiny, fast-flyers have a bold, striking color pattern. Males are gray and reddish with a red head that sports a green stripe from in front of the eye to behind the head. Hens are mottled brown. Both have a green stripe on the wing.

Calls: The females let out a high-pitched quack, while the males let out high-pitched whistles.

Similar to: blue-winged teal

Interesting facts: There are American and Eurasian versions of this teal with only slight differences. The Eurasian version shows up along the Pacific Coast from time to time.

Species: Cinnamon Teal *(see page C/11)*

Nicknames: none

Range: These are a western duck with populations heavy from California into Colorado, and a large population along the South American Pacific Coast.

In Texas: Cinnamons sometimes show up along the Texas coast, but are more common on stock tanks in the Trans-Pecos region and the Texas Hill Country.

Description: The males are a rich reddish-brown color, sometimes bordering on red-orange, and sport a black beak, red eyes, and a black undertail area. Females are mottled brown and gray. Both sexes have a blue stripe down the wings almost exactly like a blue-winged teal.

Calls: Like their green-winged cousins, the males have a high-pitched whistle while the females use a squeaky, high-pitched quack.

Similar to: The females are similar to bluewing and greenwing hens.

Interesting facts: Hunters consider these ducks one of the top trophy ducks in Texas because of their scarcity and beauty.

Species: Common Merganser *(see page C/4)*

Nicknames: fish duck

Range: They nest throughout Canada and Alaska, and winter throughout North America.

In Texas: These divers prefer open water on reservoirs, rivers, and bay systems throughout the state.

Description: The male has a black back, white sides, and mallard-green head. Females are dull gray with reddish-brown head and white on the chin.

Calls: Silent most of the year, but the males make a short grunt during courtship.

Similar to: red-breasted merganser

Interesting facts: They sometimes nest in rock crevices and rear young on the edge of cliffs.

Species: Red-Breasted Merganser *(see page C/4)*

Nicknames: fish duck, Dracula duck (that is what I call them anyway as they have fangs and red eyes)

Range: They nest throughout Canada and Alaska, and winter throughout North America.

In Texas: These divers prefer open water on reservoirs, rivers, and bay systems throughout the state. Their favorite haunts are Texas bays and tidal rivers.

Description: The male has white and gray sides, a black back, reddish-brown chest, mallard-green head, and white neck. Female are a dull gray with reddish-brown head that sports a double crest.

Calls: Silent most of the year, but the males make a short grunt during courtship.

Similar to: common merganser

Interesting facts: These are incredibly adept fish catchers that gulls sometimes follow to help them locate their next meal.

Species: Hooded Merganser *(see page C/5)*

Nicknames: hood

Range: A population exists along the Pacific Coast from southern Alaska into California. They breed and live there year-round. Most of the population is from Central Texas to the Eastern Seaboard.

In Texas: They prefer quiet, clear water. They haunt backwater ponds along the Sabine River drainage and along the coast in tidal pools in the marsh.

Description: They are about the size of a wood duck, with males being a combination of black, reddish brown, and white. The male's distinguishing characteristic is the crest that is white, bordered with black. Immature males and females appear exactly alike. They are a combination of black, gray, and brown with the neck, side, and chest gray, and head area brown. Females have a brown crest, as do immature males; not all of them have crests.

Calls: In courtship, they emit a bizarre frog-like call.

Similar to: Females are similar to red-breasted mergansers.

Interesting facts: They often compete with wood ducks for tree cavities and nest boxes. In fact, they sometimes share nests with wood ducks.

Species: Gadwall *(see page C/5)*

Nicknames: gray duck

Range: They nest throughout the Dakotas and into prairie Canada. They winter from the Eastern to Western seaboards and into Mexico.

In Texas: These ducks are likely to be anywhere and are just as comfortable in the timber as they are in coastal marsh and rice fields.

Description: Males are a combination of gray and brown with a black hind end. Females are gray-brown without the black butt area.

Calls: They let out a "reeb" type of noise.

Similar to: hen mallard, hen pintail

Interesting facts: Gadwall are famous for eyeing decoys from up high and dive-bombing them. It is truly a remarkable sight.

Species: American Widgeon *(see page C/5)*

Nicknames: baldpate widgeon (drake)

Range: They breed in the prairie pothole region of the United States on up through Alaska. They winter throughout the United States into Central America.

In Texas: You find this duck along the middle and lower Texas coasts, and on stock tanks in the Hill Country.

Description: The males of this species have bright colors with a white stripe down the head, and white flanks and underbelly. The females are a mixture of dull gray and rusty brown. Both have gray breaks with a black tip.

Calls: Females quack and the males let out a high-pitched whistle.

Similar to: Females appear similar to gadwall.

Interesting facts: Widgeon have the shortest beak of dabbling ducks, and thus are effective grazers. In some areas, they feed alongside geese in fields.

Species: Ruddy Duck *(see page C/6)*

Nicknames: butterball, bull-necked teal (Southern colloquialisms)

Range: They nest in the United States and Canadian Northwest, and winter throughout the southern half of the country and as far south as Panama.

In Texas: Ruddies most often hang out from Freeport down to Rockport in flooded fields and tidally influenced areas.

Description: The males in breeding plumage are reddish with white cheeks and a blue bill. In non-breeding plumage, the red is gray. Females are more brown with a black line through the cheek patch.

Calls: They occasionally make a popping type noise.

Similar to: female bufflehead

Interesting facts: Ruddies lay the largest eggs of any small duck. They are about the size of a wild turkey's egg.

Species: Redhead *(see page C/6)*

Nicknames: none

Range: They nest in central to western Canada and in the upper parts of the prairie pothole region. They winter in the southern United States into Mexico.

In Texas: Redheads love the bays and the largest concentrations are along the Middle and Lower Coasts in areas like Aransas Bay.

Description: The mature males have a bright red head and blue bill with a black tip. The body is gray in the middle with black ends. Females are dull reddish-brown and gray and have a dark beak.

Calls: During courtship, the males make a cat-like "meow" noise.

Similar to: canvasback

Interesting facts: The redhead may be its own worst enemy. The females lay eggs in the nests of nearly a dozen other duck species, and even the nests of bitterns. Many of these eggs fail to hatch.

Species: Canvasback *(see page C/6)*

Nicknames: bullneck, can, canard cheval, canny, canvas, gray duck, hickory-quaker, horse-duck, red-headed bullneck, sheldrake, white-back

Range: They nest in western Canada, and winter throughout the southern half of the United States.

In Texas: Canvasbacks are present on the mid-coast area, although Sabine Lake holds a fair amount in late winter.

Description: Mature males have a dark red head, distinctive ruby-red eye, and black beak. The body is light gray in the middle with black ends. Females are dull brown with a black beak and ruby-red eyes.

Calls: Males making a "coo" noise during courtship.

Similar to: redhead

Interesting facts: Canvasbacks may be the fastest flying ducks. Scientists have clocked them flying 72 miles per hour.

Species: American Black Duck *(see page C/7)*

Nicknames: black mallard

Range: Black duck nest in eastern Canada, and winter from East Texas to the Eastern Seaboard.

In Texas: Hunters sometimes kill them in the Pineywoods of East

Texas, but the birds also appear along the Gulf Coast.

Description: These large ducks are dark black and gray. Females and males appear the same, except males have a yellowish-green beak whereas females have a dingy green beak.

Calls: They make a loud "quack."

Similar to: mottled duck, female mallard.

Interesting facts: These close cousins of the mallard have a high tolerance for saltwater and love to feed in tidal pools.

Species: Black-Bellied Whistling Duck *(see page C/10)*

Nicknames: whistler, Mexican whistler, Mexican duck

Range: These ducks nest along the Texas coastline and range into Central America.

In Texas: Hunters kill a few of these in the early season along the coast and in adjoining flooded fields.

Description: These tall, long-necked ducks are light brown in color and sport a bright orange beak.

Calls: As the name implies, they make a loud whistling sound.

Similar to: fulvous whistling duck

Interesting facts: These ducks become very easily domesticated in Texas, allowing people to walk up to them during the nesting season, even if humans have never fed them.

Species: Fulvous Whistling Duck *(see page C/13)*

Nicknames: whistler

Range: A few of these ducks nest along the Texas coastline and range into Mexico. There are also populations in coastal Louisiana, Mississippi, around Mobile Bay in Alabama, and in Florida.

In Texas: Hunters kill a few during the early season, mainly along the Lower Coast.

Description: They are a long-necked duck, dull brown color, and black beak. They have a tiger-like black/brown pattern on the wings that turns to black/white in the mid-section of the body.

Calls: They make a high-pitched, loud whistle.

Similar to: black-bellied whistling duck

Interesting facts: These are not true ducks. Scientists actually classify them with geese.

Species: Canada Goose *(see page C/7)*

Nicknames: Canadian, can

Range: They nest throughout Canada and the northern United States.

In Texas: The Texas Panhandle hosts the largest migration populations of these big geese.

Description: These geese have a brownish-gray back, with a dull white underside, long black neck and head, and a white patch behind the eyes.

Calls: They make a loud, cackling "uh-rook" sound.

Similar to: Brant

Interesting facts: These geese are becoming huge pests in the Northeast, where they often nest on golf courses.

Species: Ross' Goose *(see page C/15)*

Nicknames: Ross

Range: Ross' geese nest in the Hudson Bay area, and winter along the Texas Coast and West-Central Mexico.

In Texas: They prefer fields along the Texas coast, and hang out with snow geese.

Description: They are a tiny goose with a solid white body, orange triangular-shaped bill, and orange legs and feet.

Calls: They produce a high-pitched yelping noise.

Similar to: snow goose

Interesting facts: First year Ross' geese are as dumb as a bird can get, and readily decoy. They sometimes hang out in a spread while hunters are shooting other birds. If you notice a decoy that looks suspiciously real, you might want to give it a second look.

Species: White-Fronted Goose *(see page C/16)*

Nicknames: specklebelly, speck

Range: They nest in Alaska and the tundra region of Canada, and winter in southern Texas, Mexico, and along the Pacific Coast of the United States.

In Texas: These geese love agricultural fields and can most likely be found near them along the Gulf Coast.

Description: These medium geese have a brown and gray colored body with a white belly. In mature specimens, there are large bars or speckles. They have an orange/pink bill and orange legs and feet.

Calls: They make a laughing-like sound.

Similar to: domestic goose

Interesting facts: These geese tend to mate for life and often migrate in family groups.

Species: Lesser Snow Goose *(see page C/7)*

Nicknames: white goose, blue (blue phase), eaglehead (blue phase)

Range: They nest in Arctic Canada, and winter in Texas, Mexico, southern New Mexico, and along the Pacific Coast.

In Texas: The Texas Panhandle and Gulf Coast area are full of snows. You find them in agricultural fields and sometimes in the marshes.

Description: Most are white with black wingtips and orange bill. There is also a blue phase where they are blue/gray with white mixed in. The head is usually white during this time, earning the nickname "eaglehead."

Calls: They make a "wak" type of noise.

Similar to: Ross' goose

Interesting facts: The populations have skyrocketed to the point that scientists thought they would ruin the Arctic habitat forever. Now, thanks to liberalized hunting regulations, the populations are more in check, although still being monitored.

Species: American Coot *(see page C/12)*

Nicknames: Pool d'eau, mudhen, moorhen

Range: Coots nest in the prairie pothole region of the United States into Canada. They winter throughout most of the United States.

In Texas: Coots like big water and can be found on reservoirs and on any bay or coastal marsh flat.

Description: They have a black/gray body and white/gray beak.

Calls: They make all kinds of noises, but the most common are honks, grunts, and a whinnying type of sound.

Similar to: moorhen, greeb

Interesting facts: When alarmed, coots appear as if they are running across the water as they take flight.

HYBRIDS

Some duck species, particularly mallard, are not very fussy about the species they breed. They, of course, prefer their own kind, but if a sexy pintail swims by and no one is looking, things can get heated in the prairie pothole region.

Hunters sometimes kill ducks that defy textbook description, and that is most often because they are dealing with hybrids.

The most common is the mallard/pintail hybrid. Taxidermist Bubba

Andres of Winnie has mounted several of these, and has an awesome specimen hanging in his showroom.

"Sometimes, they look more pintail, and others more mallard. This one that I have in my shop is a perfect hybrid," he said.

The duck has a body shaped like a pintail with a long neck, but has the green head of a mallard, with the grayish-blue beak of the pintail. Its feet are orange like a mallard, and its coloration is pintail-like on top. The coolest part is the tail, which is long like a pintail, but curled upward like a mallard.

Other frequent cross-breeders are mottled duck, black duck, and teal.

Domestic ducks get in the picture sometimes, and really make things weird.

I met a hunter once who shot what looked like a mallard/muscovie hybrid. It had green on top of its head, but had the weird, reddish-colored muscovie face and feathers that were a combination of black, white, gray, and brown. It was also quite fat. It was not the prettiest thing in the world, but it made a unique trophy and one heck of a conversation piece.

Considering the looks of a muscovie, there must have been one lonely mallard out there in Duckland.

Chapter Three

Waterfowl Hotspots:
The Upper Coast

The Upper Coast area where I grew up hunting is among the most challenging, treacherous regions in the state for waterfowlers. The marshes around Sabine Lake, the Keith Lake Chain, and Trinity Bay have some of the deepest gumbo mud found anywhere. I am speaking from experience, having literally pushed a boat 1/4-mile out of mud flats in navel-deep mud with the help of my cousin, Frank Moore. We felt like crying afterwards.

The good part is there are plenty of public opportunities available to waterfowlers, with a large system of national wildlife refuges, wildlife management areas, and open bays. The area also has a fair amount of prairie to hunt, but all of it with the exception of part of the Anahuac National Wildlife Refuge is private land, accessible only by leasing from a landowner or using an outfitter. These are typically the best hunting areas, as flooded rice offers much better food for puddle ducks than most of the marshes. For geese, rye grass fields in the areas around Winnie and Stowell are a huge draw.

This is the playground of hunters from the Houston and

Beaumont/Port Arthur/Orange areas. The public grounds can be crowded, so those who do the most scouting and are willing to work for their birds do the best.

Mottled duck are a common sight on marshes in the Upper Coast region. This enigmatic species nests only along the Gulf and southern Atlantic coasts.

REGIONAL STRATEGIES

Starting with the early teal season, hunters with access to semi-brackish or freshwater ponds can score in a big way. Teal blast through the area in a hurry, and if there is a water problem like there often is in September, any place that has some water and food will have teal.

If you are hunting public marsh, set up in grassy areas and put out a spread of a couple of dozen teal mixed with mallard-sized decoys. Native mottled duck are present along with wood duck and Mexican whistler, so having some larger decoys in the spread will make things look natural. For prairie hunting, you might want to consider putting out a larger spread, as the teal often flock in huge numbers in the flooded fields.

Not much calling is required for teal, although if the birds do not want to hit the decoys, using a teal whistle will often turn them around. If they are way out, you might want to use a mallard call to get their attention and then lay on the whistle.

During the regular duck season, expect most of the action during the first week and after each successive cold front to blast new ducks into the area. On the prairie, the best hunting is not when you might expect it:

"We much prefer days with lots of sunshine," said Brian Fischer, owner of Drake Plantation Outfitters. "I know that many people think of duck and goose hunting being best in terrible weather, but if we have a good wind and clear skies, they decoy much better around here. When you have high clouds, the hunting is tough. If you only have limited days to choose, pick a clear one, or if you want ducks in the prairie or marsh, rain is good because it gets them moving. Again, high cloud days are tough."

Early on, the size of the decoy spread does not matter that much, but it is important to vary them and have some pintails in the mix.

"Pintails are light-colored and they are a duck we have a lot of," said avid waterfowler—and my cousin—Frank Moore. "They tend to get the attention of ducks real well, and when you finish them off with gadwall, teal, and a few geese in the spread, you can do really well in the prairie or marsh.

"I always put out a great blue heron, too. Those herons are smart birds and ducks know that if everything is cool with them, it should be safe. Also, I sometimes throw in coots for good measure. There are lots of coots at times, especially in the Lower Neches Wildlife Management Area and surrounding marshes."

The bays in the region offer some good hunting opportunities as well.

For hunters wanting to target geese in the region, particularly on the refuges, it is important to learn their flyways.

Refuge geese are creatures of habit compared to some of those roosting on nearby private lands. There are more constants on the refuge and the geese that migrate there tend to get into more of a reliable pattern. What a hunter has to do is to pay serious attention to where the geese are flying to and from, and what time they tend to get up and move.

Specklebelly geese prefer the flooded fields in the region. Here, Shane Chesson (left) and Brian Fischer, both of Drake Plantation Outfitters, discuss a banded bird while Shane's lab, Remy, looks on.

Getting up early in the morning and expecting the geese to fly at dawn is not necessarily something hunters should expect. Quite often, the best flight is around 10 a.m., when many hunters are already heading back home frustrated with the lack of action. These geese are not stupid. They have figured out the patterns of the hunters much better than hunters have figured out the pattern of the geese. Wait for the late shooting action because, more often than not, it pays off.

The recommended dose of decoys on the refuges is not what many hunters would consider adequate for these wary geese, which tend to get up off the roost by the thousands in the area. A lot of guys put out hundreds, maybe even a thousand, but it is not necessary if you focus more on moving decoys. Plus, it is hard for a couple of hunters to put out that many early in the morning. Put out about half a dozen kites if the wind is adequate, as well as several decoys with moving wings, and carry a black flag to wave at the birds. Finish off the spread by putting out a couple of dozen magnum-sized decoys in small clusters, and do minimal calling. I think many times snows are going to commit whether or not we call, and with an older population of birds like we have on the Upper Coast, they can be very call shy, especially later in the season.

Well-informed local hunters have learned to watch the weather forecast for heavy fog, a bringer of super snow goose hunting opportunity. This is almost exclusively a proposition of pass shooting the geese as they fly low, confused in the thick, misty blanket. The key is targeting the levees and ridges in the refuge system that low flying geese use as roadways as they slowly cruise heading to and from feeding areas. This is the time for calling once the geese get close, luring them even closer for a shot.

Ryan Warhola of Port Acres has had good success bagging these low flying geese, and emphasized that hunters need to be very mindful of weather conditions: "You have to really pay attention to the weather and be prepared to leave at the last minute, because this is a matter of keying in on confused geese, and that's something you don't get a chance to do every day."

Warhola recommended that hunters get familiar with the flight patterns of the birds in the section of the refuge they want to hunt: "Find some good cover, like around a levee or just behind a small ridge, and use that as your signpost for shooting and calling. Once the birds get to your spot, let them have it with all barrels. If the fog is high enough that you can see a fair way up, you'll want to take farther shots, but if it's really thick, you can make super high percentage shots at near point-blank range."

Finding good cover and waiting for flyover geese is a good option on refuges. Here, Michael Cascio of Orange blends in perfectly with his surroundings.

PUBLIC HUNTING HOTSPOTS

Area: Sabine Lake

Location: Jefferson and Orange counties

Primary Species: scaup, teal, pintail, bufflehead

Hotspots: The best areas on this lake are on the north end. Hickory Cove, which borders the Hawk Club to the north and the Lower Neches Wildlife Management Area to the west, is an expansive open-water area. At times, it can hold fair to good numbers of pintail and offers shooting at teal and other puddle ducks trading from the north and west to Louisiana marshes to the east, and vice versa. The main lake around the islands holds good numbers of scaup and bufflehead that like to hang around between the mouth of East Pass and the Intracoastal Canal.

Special Regulations: Texas and Louisiana co-own this body of water. There is a reciprocal agreement between the states regarding to fishing, where anglers can fish all of the main shorelines but cannot enter any cuts without the other state's license. This does not extend to hunting. If you are hunting along the Louisiana shoreline, you must have a Louisiana hunting license.

Notes: This is some of the toughest coastal bottom in the country to walk. You definitely want a dog to hunt here. Also, there are no blinds like there are on other Texas bays. You will have to hunt out of your boat and camouflage it well to be successful here.

Area: Lower Neches Wildlife Management Area

Location: Orange County just outside of Bridge City

Primary Species: teal, gadwall, shoveler, mottled duck, scaup

Hotspots: This refuge is broken into two units: the Old River and Nelda Stark. The Old River Unit divides into the West and East Side.

The author holds his hunting party's group of ducks and geese taken in Chambers County.

The East Side, which offers walk-in and boat access, has its best hunting in the northeast corner in some of the larger ponds accessible only by a super-shallow-running boat. The West Side can offer good hunting in front of the terrace islands off Highway 87, and in some of the ponds on the Bessie Heights Marsh side. The Nelda Stark Unit is not as consistent, but is good on weekends when nearby hunting pushes birds to this far less pressured area.

Special Regulations: Hunters must possess a valid Annual Public Hunting permit. Shooting hours at the Old River Unit end at noon, and at the close of legal shooting time at the Nelda Stark Unit. Permitted users may enter the property after 4:30 a.m. Temporary blinds may be constructed using only natural vegetation; no permanent blinds are permitted.

Notes: The Nelda Stark Unit is one of the only management areas that offers evening hunting. Texas Parks & Wildlife Department officials did that so hunters in the region would have a place to hunt after work. The west side of the Old River Unit runs right along Highway 87. While there are no official rules for how far hunters should be off the road, but I spoke with law enforcement officials that said it would be a good idea for hunters to be at least 50 yards from Highway 87. For more information, call 409-736-2551.

Area: J.D. Murphree Wildlife Management Area

Location: Jefferson County near the towns of Port Acres and Sabine Pass

Primary Species: gadwall, teal, pintail, shoveler, mottled duck, snow geese

Hotspots: The Salt Bayou Unit offers what can be some excellent hunting in the distant area of the Keith Lake Chain in Johnson Lake and Shell Lake.

Special Regulations: Hunters can access this refuge with an Annual Public Hunting permit or $15 daily permit available from refuge headquarters. For regular permit hunts, check in is at 4:30 a.m.

Compartments will be assigned at the time of registration. An Annual Public Hunting permit is required for special goose season dates. The use of airboats is prohibited, except in Big Hill Bayou, Blind Bayou, and Keith Lake. Airboats of 10 horsepower or less may be used for access by only permitted waterfowl hunters within that portion of the area located south of the Intracoastal Waterway on designated waterfowl hunt days.

Notes: This area is the gauge by which Upper Coast waterfowl hunting is measured, as it has a variety of habitat and many hunters. Expect long lines during the first few weeks of the season and around the opening of the second split. For more information, call 409-736-2551.

Hunters should be cautious using dogs in the early teal season. In fact, the author recommends not using them at all in the marsh in September. Here, guide Harlan Hatcher tries to run a gator off a road on a ranch near Winnie during November 2005, when the temperature was in the 40s. The gator was out catching some rays and did not want to move, but finally obliged.

41

Area: Sea Rim State Park

Location: Jefferson County near Sabine Pass

Primary Species: teal, gadwall, pintail, scaup, shoveler, merganser

Hotspots: There is not one spot here that can be considered a "hotspot." Sea Rim is small; when it is on, it is on—and when it is not, it is not.

Special Regulations: Hunters may enter the hunt area after 4:30 a.m. on designated hunt days, and must be off park grounds by noon. Hunters must possess an Annual Public Hunting permit and park vehicles in designated numbered parking sites for the numbered hunting site used. The area is small and can accommodate only four parties on a first-come, first-served basis.

Notes: Access is by foot only and requires walking about 1/2-mile through the marsh. As walk-in access goes, this area is about as good as it gets. When the hunting is strong, Sea Rim can provide excellent action for hunters who do not have a boat, or simply feel like trying something different.

Area: McFaddin National Wildlife Refuge

Location: Jefferson County near Sabine Pass

Primary Species: Teal, scaup, mottled duck, gadwall, shoveler, snow geese

Hotspots: Some of the favorite areas of hunters are the Mud Lake Unit and any of the spots in the Spaced Hunt area.

Special Regulations: All hunters must have a signed general permit. There is free access to the Central Hunt Unit east and west of White Levee. Another free hunt area is the Star Lake/Clam Lake Unit. During the regular waterfowl season only, all hunters in the Star Lake/Clam Lake Hunt Units must register at the check station, including those accessing the unit from the beach along the brine line or from Perkins Levee. All hunters accessing Star Lake and associated waters via boat must access through the refuge

Several of the refuges and management areas in the region offer easy walk-in access. This is a walkway onto a levee at the Lower Neches Wildlife Management Area.

Star Lake boat ramp. The Mud Lake Unit offers free access, some by walk-in via the beach and some boat-in access from the Intracoastal Canal along the Jefferson/Chambers County Line. The Spaced Hunt Unit requires a $10 daily fee. Refuge officials will give permits to registered hunters beginning at 4:00 a.m. the day of the hunt at the waterfowl check station. Spaced Hunt areas not claimed by 5:00 a.m. will go to standby hunters on a first-come, first-served basis. Refuge officials take reservations for Fee Area Hunt Permits between 8:00 a.m. and 11:30 a.m. the Friday before the hunt week. Reservations go alternately between hunters present at the check station and telephone callers. Permits are yours until 5:00 a.m. the day of hunt. For phone reservations, call 409-971-0337. Airboats may not exceed 10 horsepower with direct drive, have a propeller length of 48 inches or less, and engines may not exceed two cylinders and 484cc. Motorized boats powered by air cooled or radiator-cooled engines are restricted to those powered by a single engine of 25 horsepower or less and utilizing a propeller 9 inches in diameter or less. No other motorized vehicles permitted. The minimum distance between hunt parties is 200 yards.

Notes: The Spaced Hunt area at Pond 11 is for disabled hunters. It will become available to non-disabled hunt parties only on a standby basis at 5:00 a.m. on each hunt day. If any disabled parties arrive for standby status, Pond 11 will go to that party. This is a treacherous marsh with severely deep mud. It is one you definitely want to have a dog to hunt, and never hunt alone. For more information, call 409-971-2909.

Area: Texas Point National Wildlife Refuge

Location: Jefferson County near Sabine Pass

Primary Species: teal, shoveler, scaup, pintail, gadwall

Hotspots: Some of the flats off Texas Bayou can be hot for puddle ducks. Remote ponds accessible to brave souls who do not mind a good walk can hold good numbers of teal in the early season.

If a decoy spread is not working, don't be afraid to get out and rearrange things.

Special Regulations: All hunters must have a signed general permit. Access is available by walk-in from Highway 87. Boat-in access is available only through Texas Bayou. Airboats may not exceed 10 horsepower with direct drive and a propeller length of 48 inches or less, and engines may not exceed two cylinders and 484cc. Motorized boats powered by air-cooled or radiator-cooled engines are restricted to those powered by a single engine of 25 horsepower or less and utilizing a propeller 9 inches in diameter or less. No other motorized vehicles permitted. The minimum distance between hunt parties is 200 yards.

Notes: This is probably the most underrated public hunting area on the Upper Coast. The hunting here is difficult due to the terrain, but hunters who find the flyways within the refuge can score big time. For more information, call 409-971-2909.

Area: Trinity Bay

Location: Chambers and Harris counties

Primary Species: Shovelers, pintail, gadwall, scaup

Hotspots: The north shoreline is probably the most consistent area to kill ducks.

Special Regulations: Just remember that if hunting out of a boat, you must be in an anchored position.

Notes: The hunting on Trinity Bay tends to heat up when the hunting in the nearby marshes slows down, especially for divers and pintail, which like dabbling along the shallow shorelines.

Area: Anahuac National Wildlife Refuge

Location: Chambers County near the towns of Anahuac and Hankamer

Primary Species: teal, gadwall, mottled duck, pintail, shoveler, snow geese, specklebelly

A good retriever is a must while hunting the silt-laden bays and marsh on the Upper Coast. These bays are extremely tough to wade in many of the best duck hunting areas.

Hotspots: The East Unit probably offers the best hunting, which is likely the reason behind the fee to hunt there as opposed to the other units.

Special Regulations: All hunters must have a signed general permit. There is free access to approximately 3000 acres in the Pace and Middleton Tracts. The East Unit is available to hunters with an Annual Public Hunting permit or for a $10 daily fee. Hunters may enter the refuge units no earlier than 4:00 a.m. Hunting starts at legal shooting time and closes at noon. Hunters must be off the refuge by 12:30 p.m. Hunters should note that on inland waters of the refuge, the use of motorized boats is restricted to lakes, ponds, ditches, and other waterways. The operation of motorized boats on or through emergent wetland vegetation is illegal. Refuge officials restrict the use of boats powered by air-cooled or radiator-cooled engines to those powered by a single engine of 25 horsepower or less and utilizing a propeller 9 inches in diameter or less. All airboats, marsh buggies, ATVs, and personal watercraft are illegal. Portable blinds or temporary native vegetation blinds are legal, but hunters must take them down after a hunt. The minimum distance between hunt parties is 200 yards.

Notes: The East Unit has a special goose hunting area on the agricultural part of the refuge in a Spaced Hunt area. Hunters in this area must have goose decoys. Individuals in each group must set up and stay in their permitted area and stay within 50 feet of each other during the hunt unless retrieving geese. For more information, call 409-267-3337.

The Anahuac National Wildlife Refuge offers some excellent goose hunting on an agricultural area of the refuge.

Area: Sabine Surf

Location: Jefferson County out of Sabine Pass

Primary Species: scaup, hooded merganser, bufflehead

Hotspots: The best area is the shallow flats just off the beach beyond the Texas Point National Wildlife Refuge.

Special Regulations: This is public access, but hunters should beware that they must have their anchor out while hunting from a boat.

Notes: This is not a place where you will have the hunt of your life. However, it is a spot hardly anyone hunts and offers a shot at some hard to find species like hooded merganser and bufflehead. When pressure gets heavy at Texas Point, some of the ducks will trade out into the surf, so you will occasionally shoot some puddle ducks.

Chapter four

Waterfowl Hotspots:
The Middle Coast

The Middle Coast region arguably provides the most consistent hunting for the largest variety of species in the state. Species that collectors find hard to get, such as redhead, bufflehead, and even goldeneye are present in this region. Hunting centers on, in, and around shallow bays.

The region has an almost overwhelming amount of opportunities for waterfowlers, but the shallowness of the bays makes access problematic at times. Major cold fronts compound this, as they turn skinny water to mud flats.

The boat of choice here is an airboat, which is loud and obtrusive, but allows hunters to get into the hard to reach areas such as freshwater ponds in the marshes, and lightly pressured zones that hold the most birds.

BEST REGIONAL STRATEGIES

The secret to bagging ducks here is to think big.

A decoy spread in a marsh pond might consist of two dozen. On open water, the starting number is six dozen, with some hunters putting out as many as 200.

Capt. Skip James knows more about open-water duck hunting than anyone I have met. He spent 20 years hunting ducks on open waters around the country, and is a big believer in putting out lots of decoys.

Hunting open water over lots of decoys is common practice along the Middle Coast region of the state.

"If you're putting out anything less than 100, you're cheating yourself," James said. "Ducks congregate in big numbers on open water, especially redheads and bluebills [scaup]. You have to mimic nature to get nature to cooperate with you, and that means going through the trouble of putting out a bunch of decoys."

James also believes that, when it comes to decoys, bigger is truly better. Besides mimicking nature, you have to get the duck's attention, and using big decoys is a way to do that: "When a duck is flying around over open water, which is often choppy, it may have a hard time seeing regular size

The author photographed this huge mixed flock of redhead and pintail while hunting in Aransas Bay. The big waters of the Middle Coast area draw big numbers of ducks, so a larger decoy spread that mimics a big flock is popular with hunters.

decoys or a small spread. Think big and you will have success."

Some hunters mix in a half-dozen or so snow goose imitations to help draw attention, particularly later in the season. White shows up well on chocolate-colored Texas bays, and occasionally helps draw a few bonus geese.

"This time of year, ducks are showing all of their colors. There is a lot of white out there in the sky, and it seems to be seen at greater distances," James said.

Many hunters set their decoys in a large cove, leave a landing area, and extend one long leg of the spread out into open water to attract cruising ducks. This is highly effective, especially if you have a couple of mechanical duck decoys with rotating wings.

Islands, which are omnipresent in the bays in this region, are good spots to hunt. The prime spot is toward the tail of an island, in the soft water between the tail and the main current.

Usually the best duck shooting time is early and after 9 a.m. when the birds return to the main bay after a morning feed in the marsh. Ducks typically trade back-and-forth and up-and-down the marsh most of the early morning, then there is a lull as they feed in fields, and then another burst of activity in late morning.

Jess Curlew of Corpus Christi targets the main points of bays early in the morning, and said ducks are highly patternable: "When the ducks are coming off the bay to feed out toward the marsh, they usually enter at a point, or at least the biggest flocks do. Conversely, ducks leaving the marsh to go toward the bay follow points as well. I don't know what it is about these areas, but they serve as a sort of travel route for ducks."

Curlew likes to start his spreads with what he calls the "water droplet" or "teardrop" layout: "This consists of decoys set up in the shape of a water droplet with one end tapering off sharply. You can camouflage the boat greatly and set up in the middle of the set, or hunt just off of the edges."

A set commonly used in northern states and favored by Curlew is the "wings" layout, which consists of one big mass of regular-sized decoys with two thin strips of magnums coming off the side: "This spread is also huntable from inside the layout, but it's probably best to camouflage up and hunt the outside edges where the birds come from. This will allow you to get a shot in before the birds flare up and leave."

As with all saltwater pursuits, be mindful of the tides. Low tide decreases the amount of water available to ducks and makes them fly as the water recedes from the marsh. High tides provide access to areas unavailable when waters are low. A hunter must know when he can enter these areas and when he must exit before the tide falls and leaves him stranded.

Wind, too, can dictate where a hunter can hunt safely, as well as where the best hunting spots are. Ducks prefer to feed and rest on the lee side of islands and points.

Goose hunting in the region centers around the abundant agriculture, and finding consistent success is a matter of staying on what the geese are eating.

"They might be in the rice stubble real heavy, and then move onto rye grass at the drop of a hat," said veteran Middle Coast goose hunter Roger Craig. "If you don't have access to where the geese are feeding, you have to try to lure them to you, which with snows in particular, is getting more difficult by the year."

Craig recommended that hunters set up on geese with a barrage of decoys for the best chance at success: "Set up a minimum of a thousand

Snow geese in the region receive heavy pressure and hunters must pursue them almost as if they were whitetail deer with good camouflage and little movement by hunters.

decoys and mix it up with rags, shells, kites, and standing decoys. Make sure and vary species, too. You'll want snows, blues, and throw a few specklebellies or Canadas in there as well."

As far calling, Craig recommended doing it as much as possible: "I'm big on calling for geese. It gets hard to get these creatures to commit, so if you have the skills to make realistic goose calls, by all means do it."

Craig is also big on camouflage: "Snows are wary everywhere, but down on this part of the coast we get after them a lot, and they seem to be even a little more shy to odd colors. Make sure to match your surroundings and never go without face paint or a mask. That's a big no-no in my book. You have to take all precautions if you want to score."

PUBLIC HUNTING HOTSPOTS

Area: Peach Point Wildlife Management Area

Location: Brazoria County

Primary species: teal, shoveler, gadwall, mottled duck

Hotspots: The mottled duck marsh and greenwing impoundment are typically the more popular areas with local hunters.

Special Regulations: Provisions require that all boats must be hand launched and only electric motors used. Gates open two hours before legal shooting time, and hunters must check in and out. Check out time is noon. To access this area, hunters must have an Annual Public Hunting Permit or purchase a $15 regular daily permit.

Contact: Todd Merendino, 979-244-6804.

Area: Mad Island Wildlife Management Area

Location: Matagorda County

Primary species: green-winged teal, black-bellied whistling duck, mottled duck, scaup

Hotspots: Hunters should target any of the deeper ponds in the area, as they attract both puddle ducks and divers.

Special Regulations: Gates open two hours before legal shooting time, and hunters must check in and out. Check out time is noon. To access this area, hunters must have an Annual Public Hunting Permit or purchase a $15 regular daily permit.

Contact: Todd Merendino, 979-244-6804

Area: Brazoria National Wildlife Refuge

Location: Brazoria County

Primary species: pintail, widgeon, gadwall, teal, shoveler, snow geese

Hotspots: The backwaters in the Christmas Point area as well as the main shoreline of the bay

Special Regulations: No special permit is required to hunt this area. Use of the area is on a first-come, first-serve basis. Hunters can use non-motorized bicycles along Alligator Road when hunting the Middle Bayou Public Hunting Area, as well as airboats in navigable tidal waters. No hunting within 500 feet of houses.

Notes: When hunting on the open waters of this refuge, consider mixing in some goose decoys, as there are quite a few snows that roost in the area and you might just get a few to come in for a closer look.

Contact: Refuge headquarters, 979-849-6062

Area: San Bernard National Wildlife Refuge

Location: Brazoria County

Primary species: pintail, shoveler, teal, scaup, snow geese, widgeon

Hotspots: Any time a refuge has permitted and non-permitted areas, you can bet the ones you have to get a permit for are the better hunting zones. This is true in the case of this refuge.

Special Regulations: No permits are required for the public hunting areas of this refuge. They *are* required for the Sargent and Big Pond Waterfowl Hunt. Reservations for these hunts are available by contacting the main office. Access to the public hunting areas is by public waterways. A refuge boat ramp is available on Cedar Creek Lake for small boats. No ATVs are allowed on the refuge at any time.

Notes: This is a highly overlooked hunting area and is close enough to Houston for hunters to easily access.

Contact: Refuge headquarters, 979-849-7771

Area: Guadalupe Delta Wildlife Management Area (Hynes Bay Unit)

Location: Refugio County

Hunting divers on the bays is tough without a dog. Wounded redhead in particular are bad about diving down and popping about 50 yards away. Chasing them down on foot is no fun. With that said, a special note of caution for hunters is to shuffle your feet while walking in the bays. Stingrays are present here, sometimes even during winter. The author almost stepped on one while putting out decoys in the winter of 2005.

Primary species: teal, shoveler, widgeon, mottled duck, canvasback, pintail, widgeon

Hotspots: The harder to access ponds in the Townsend Bayou area are the best to target.

Special Regulations: Hunters must possess an Annual Public Hunting Permit. They can enter the property after 4:00 a.m. Scouting is only legal the day before the teal season opener and the day before each split of the season. All hunters must be off refuge property 1/2 hour after sunset. Hunters must park in the designated numbered parking area for the numbered hunting site used.

Notes: This area is open to special permit hunting only.

Contact: Texas Parks & Wildlife Department, 361-552-6637

Area: Guadalupe Delta Wildlife Management Area (Guadalupe River Unit)

Location: Refugio County

Primary species: teal, shoveler, widgeon, mottled duck, canvasback, widgeon

Hotspots: Target the most secluded spots with good cover and enough water to survive a major cold front.

Special Regulations: Hunters must possess an Annual Public Hunting Permit. They can enter the property after 4:00 a.m. Scouting is only legal the day before the teal season opener and each split of the season. All hunters must be off refuge property 1/2 hour after sunset. Waterfowl hunters must park in the designated numbered parking area for the numbered hunting site used.

Notes: This area can be red hot during the early teal season. Bluewings get thick in the area, especially after they have blasted through the Upper Coast region.

Contact: Texas Parks & Wildlife Department, 361-552-6637

Area: Big Boggy National Wildlife Refuge

Location: Brazoria County near Angleton

Primary species: teal, shoveler, widgeon, mottled duck, canvasback

Hotspots: Hunters accessing the more remote areas of the refuge along the Intracoastal Waterway typically report better success and a wider variety of species.

Special Regulations: Access is by boat along the Gulf Intracoastal Waterway and by land on Chinquapin Road. There is no ATV travel allowed within refuge boundaries. The dredge disposal areas along the Gulf Intracoastal Waterway are not open to public hunting due to safety hazards. Hunters cannot use permanent blinds so as to prevent any special claims to portions of this public hunting area. Use of the area is strictly on a first-come, first-served basis. Hunters must maintain a "safe and courteous" distance from other parties. Hunters must bring out decoys and portable blinds daily. It is important to note that retrieval of downed game from closed areas is illegal.

Notes: Look for the best hunting on this area to be during the second split of the season.

Contact: Refuge headquarters, 979-849-6062

Area: Matagorda Island Wildlife Management Area

Location: Calhoun County

Primary species: pintail, canvasback, teal, merganser, gadwall

Hotspots: The freshwater ponds on the area are magnets for ducks when they are holding water.

Special Regulations: All hunters are required to check in and out. Hunters must possess an Annual Public Hunting Permit (APH Permit) or may purchase the $15 Regular Permit (daily) at the area during check-in. The $15 Regular Permit fee is not necessary for persons possessing the APH Permit or for supervised minors. Hunters can access the interior freshwater ponds only on scheduled dates and at scheduled times.

Noisy airboats running across the bays during late morning can be a blessing for duck hunters, as they kick up big rafts of ducks and get them moving around.

Notes: This is a wild, relatively untamed area where you will see lots of wildlife in addition to great waterfowling. The hunter check station on the island is approximately 11 water miles from the mainland and takes about 45 minutes to reach, according to Texas Parks & Wildlife Department officials. Hunting is legal in the Bayside Marsh Unit, but hunters should be mindful that whooping cranes—a protected, endangered species—frequent the vicinity.

Contact: Texas Parks & Wildlife Department, 361-883-2215

Area: Matagorda Bay

Location: Matagorda and Calhoun Counties

Primary species: scaup, pintail, ringneck, gadwall, teal, redhead, widgeon

Hotspots: Target the points of the bay with cuts that lead into the marsh. If you can pinpoint freshwater ponds on the marsh and find the flyway of ducks, you will be well ahead of the game.

Special Regulations: N/A

Notes: Beware of whooping cranes that sometimes show up in the area. You do not want to be seen anywhere near someone shooting one of these endangered birds.

Contact: Circle H Outfitters, 281-535-1930

Area: Aransas Bay

Location: Aransas County

Primary species: redhead, pintail, scaup, bufflehead, teal

Hotspots: The duck hunting on the bay here revolves around the seagrass beds. Target the open, shallow water around the seagrass beds for best success, especially on redhead.

Special Regulations: The only special waterfowl regulation here is that sandhill cranes are not legal to harvest due to the presence of whooping cranes.

Notes: If you want to shoot a redhead in Texas, this is the place to go. If you do not shoot

Cinnamon teal occasionally show up on this end of the coast. Here, Ducks Unlimited Texas fundraising guru David Schuessler shows off a drake shot while hunting with W.L. Sherrill's guide service near Wharton.

The author, right, shares a photo opportunity with legendary call maker and duck hunting video host Buck Gardner on Aransas Bay. They bagged a nice mixed limit of redhead, pintail, scaup, bufflehead, and gadwall.

birds early, hang around for a while. When the airboats start moving around the bay to pick up hunters, they will push the birds off the main bay and you will probably get a shot.

Contact: Shoal Grass Lodge, 866-758-5307

Area: Lavaca Bay

Location: Calhoun County

Primary species: redhead, pintail, shoveler, mottled duck, scaup

Hotspots: This area is famous for its flats, which draw large numbers of ducks.

Special Regulations: The only special waterfowl regulation here is that sandhill cranes are not legal to harvest due to the presence of whoop-

Goose hunters in the region need to be flexible and willing to do a lot of scouting if they wish to be successful.

ing cranes.

Notes: This Lavaca Bay area is a highly overlooked area for duck hunting, and offers a wide variety of species.

Contact: Capt. Kris Kelley, 361-785-2587

QUEST FOR BUFFLEHEAD ENDS ON MIDDLE COAST

I have been on a quest to bag bufflehead since the 2000-2001 hunting season. Back then, my cousin, Frank Moore, and I were hunting out on Lake Sabine, and kept having buffleheads buzz our decoys. The tiny, attractively patterned ducks would fly past the outer edge of decoys just out of shooting range. They frustrated us to no end and inspired us to figure out ways to get them to decoy.

We experimented with different decoy patterns, big spreads, small spreads, and I even painted a few teal decoys to look like a bufflehead, all to no avail.

By the end of the season, we said our hunting goal was to get a pair of buffleheads even if it meant forsaking all other ducks.

Some might wonder what the fascination is with a duck that few hunters pursue. Well, we both are fans of duck taxidermy, and eventually want to get one of each species for our collections. In addition, I think we felt like after having these beautiful birds tease us so many times, we just had to see what they tasted like in a gumbo.

In December 2005, we hunted a few hundred yards from our old haunt on the north end of Lake Sabine, and ended up wading in mud up to our chests. We saw bufflehead, but once again, they refused to decoy. A few weeks later, I got to hunt with Shoal Grass Lodge in Aransas Pass with legendary duck caller and call manufacturer Buck Gardner. We ended up limiting out while hunting a seagrass flat near an island in Aransas Bay, taking pintail, redhead, and widgeon.

About halfway through our hunt, I looked behind us to see a bufflehead hen cupping her wings in preparation to land in the spread. Before she hit the water, I hit her with some No. 3 shot.

I finally got a bufflehead!

My ultimate goal was a drake, but I figured I could save the hen and get it mounted if I were to get a drake one day.

Thirty minutes later, I look up and see a gorgeous bufflehead drake buzzing the edge of the decoys. It was too far out to make a clean shot, so I put down my shotgun. Then the bird turned and dove right down toward our spread. Before it could hit the water, I squeezed the trigger and ended a five-year quest.

I felt like a little kid at Christmas.

Since Frank and I began our quest, I logged well over 100 hunts, went through several cases of steel shot, and waded through acres of chest deep mud, rice fields, and even three feet of snow in the Sierra Nevada Mountains in California. During these hunts, I took mallard,

The author bagged these bufflehead in January 2006, ending a five-year quest to score a pair.

PHOTO BY BUCK GARDNER

gadwall, pintail, teal, widgeon, scaup, ringneck, shoveler, specklebelly, Canadian geese, and snows, and had some amazing times. However, none of those were as exciting as taking those two bufflehead on Aransas Bay.

This experience just goes to show, whether it is a mallard, big whitetail buck, or lunker largemouth that gets your heart pumping, it does not matter. All that matters is that you travel beyond the pavement and embrace the wild. Along the way, you might find your own "bufflehead." If you do, count yourself lucky.

Chapter five

Waterfowl Hotspots:
The Lower Coast

The lower southern third of the Texas coast is most widely known for its deer and nilgai antelope hunting. However, there is some top-notch duck hunting here.

The monstrous King and Kennedy ranches own much of the land along the Gulf. A good portion of what is not theirs is controlled by the federal government as part of the national wildlife refuge system, and no waterfowl hunting is allowed.

Yes, hunting is supposed to be a "priority" use of refuge land, but not necessarily waterfowl hunting. You can read a lot more about this in the final chapter of this book.

For hunters interested in this region, it can provide some excellent shooting opportunities, including the chance to bag a couple of species rarely taken in other areas of the state. Black-bellied whistling and fulvous tree ducks are present down here, both of which are fine tasting and beautiful birds. If you happen to hunt down in this region, be sure to bring along a good whistling call. These birds are relatively easy to lure into shooting range.

"If I can get a whistler within 100 yards, I can usually call it in," said duck hunting veteran Roger Blakely of Brownsville. "They are slow-flying ducks so it might seem like they are not interested, but if you keep at it, they will make their way toward you more often than not. That is, if you can make a good whistle like them."

Blakely noted that black-bellied tree ducks mate for life, and if you get one bird down, keep calling because the mate will usually come back.

"If you get one of a pair, chances are you will get the other if you are persistent with your calling and stay still," he said.

Hunters should also be aware of the presence of masked ducks, or Mexican masked ducks, as hunters sometimes call them. These tiny ducks are very similar in appearance to the ruddy duck, but are much more rare. They

PHOTO COURTESY OF THE U.S. FISH AND WILDLIFE SERVICE

Black-bellied whistling ducks or "Mexican whistlers" are present in fair numbers along the Lower Coast. These unique ducks are actually closer akin to geese.

are definitely a bird to send to the taxidermist if you get one.

Hunters should typically set up as they would for bay hunting on the Upper and Middle Coasts. Big spreads are best to lure in redheads, canvasbacks, and other open-water lovers common in the region.

This is a region to be very mindful of the tides, as most of these areas are very, very shallow. Tides are a blessing and a curse to bay hunters in the region. Tides can move ducks to hunters, or leave boats high and dry. There is nothing worse than trying to get a boat out of a mud flat in the winter. I have done it on two occasions, and can tell you it sucks.

Low tide decreases the amount of water available to ducks and makes them fly as the water recedes from the marsh. High tides, on the other hand, provide access to areas unavailable when waters are low. A hunter must know when he can enter these areas and when he must exit before the tide falls and leaves him stranded.

Wind, too, can dictate where a hunter can hunt safely, as well as where the best hunting spots are. Ducks prefer to feed and rest on the lee side of islands and points, and those are the key habitat in which hunters in the region find the most success.

Hunting in the super shallow bay systems in the region is dictated by the tides. Pay special attention to tidal charts and weather conditions before planning a hunt.

PUBLIC HUNTING HOTSPOTS

Area: Corpus Christi Bay

Location: Just outside the big city of Corpus Christi

Primary species: redhead, scaup, pintail, widgeon

Hotspots: The southern reaches of the bay around the Oso Bay entrance

Special Regulations: Be mindful of the redhead and pintail limits and be able to identify hens early. Hens of both species look a lot like other dark-colored ducks, so you could get yourself in trouble if you are not careful.

Hunting on the big, open water in places like South Bay requires good camouflage, including face masks and gloves.

Notes: Game wardens commonly inspect boat launches that duck hunters frequent, so make sure to have your ducks divided up, and of course stay within the limits.

Contact: Capt. George Foulds, 361-729-3214

Area: Nueces Bay

Location: At the mouth of the Nueces River in the northern section of the Corpus Christi Bay complex

Primary species: redheads, scaup, pintail, widgeon, teal

Hotspots: The north shoreline and islands

Special Regulations: N/A

Notes: Expect to bag a few more puddle ducks here than you would on Corpus Christi Bay.

Contact: Green Hornet Guide Service, 361-790-9742

Area: Baffin Bay

Location: South of Kingsville

Primary species: redhead, pintail, widgeon, bufflehead

Hotspots: The north and south shorelines

Special Regulations: Be careful not to enter the surrounding lands of the big ranches in the area. They do not appreciate trespassers and will prosecute.

Notes: Be very careful navigating this bay system, as there are rock mounds created by ancient worms that are extremely hazardous to the health of your boat. Keep your eyes out for nilgai antelope that frequently run the shorelines in the area. These huge imports from India are quite a sight.

Contact: Capt. Kevin Akin, 361-949-2252.

Most of the blinds found in the region are encrusted with barnacles. For a hunter coming from inland areas, it might seem strange, but for coastal bay hunters, it is the norm.

Area: South Bay

Location: Near Port Isabel along the Mexican border corridor

Primary species: redhead, pintail, black-bellied whistling duck, fulvous tree duck, scaup

Hotspots: This is a small bay system and there is not much difference from one spot to another.

Special Regulations: N/A

Notes: There is not much information available for hunting this area. Duck hunting is done here, but it is not as popular as it is just a little way north.

Contact: Capt. Robert Sirvello, 956-943-1010

Chapter Six

Waterfowl Hotspots:
Hill Country

The Texas Hill Country is known around the world for its superior hunting, particularly in the Edwards Plateau region. It boasts the largest whitetail deer herd anywhere in the world along with an impressive collection of Rio Grande turkey, dove, quail and exotics. However, the region however is *not* known for its duck hunting, and that is a shame. There are lots of ducks in the area, although the numbers in the wintering population over the last few years is unknown. TPWD officials did not survey the Hill Country or Big Bend regions during their midwinter surveys in 2004 and 2005, so there is a big question mark over the population status.

Much of the hunting in the region is done over ponds on deer leases, where hunters just can't resist bagging some of those mallards they see on the way to the tower stands. A few years back, I was hunting on a day lease in Llano County, and the area I hunted was near a large pond. The first morning, I watched several dozen widgeon, teal, and gadwall land right along the water edge. This put me in quite a difficult position, as I had paid to hunt deer, but to be honest, I was much more interested in the ducks. I had no decoys or calls, but I did have a shotgun that I brought in case we found some quail. I dug around my truck and found a half dozen No. 4 steel shot loads and made myself a deal.

Stock tanks on Central Texas ranches can hold good numbers of ducks that receive very little pressure from hunters.

If I bagged a deer that evening, I would creep over toward the pond and try to set up where the ducks had been landing. As luck would have it, a big doe showed up about 3 p.m., so I put the crosshairs of my .243 in the middle of its neck, squeezed the trigger, dropped the doe in its tracks, and started plotting how to get those ducks.

After field dressing the doe, I took out my 12-gauge, loaded it up, and sneaked over to the pond. Just as I was about to ease down on the edge of a big live oak on the north bank of the pond, I jumped a pair of green-winged teal.

Both fell to the water after two shots.

An hour later, a big group of ringnecks came in and I whacked two of them. It was easy to tell these ducks had never been shot at on this pond, as they attempted lighting at point blank range. If ducks were this dumb where I typically hunt in the marshes of Southeast Texas, we would shoot them into extinction!

About 15 minutes before dark, I heard a familiar quacking sound. A big mallard drake was heading right in my direction, but instead of waiting until it got right on top of me as it normally would have, I snapped off two shots that were so bad I considered sticking my head in the sand like an ostrich. It was embarrassing even though I was the only "spectator."

I was lucky there was a good north wind blowing, and it pushed the ducks I had killed up against some reeds on the edge of the pond, where I was able to retrieve them with a long stick.

Back at hunting camp, all of my buddies just shook their heads and commented that only I would come back with a deer and ducks and be happier about the ducks.

That, I could not deny.

Pond hunting in the Hill Country can really pay off if you are prepared with some decoys, a couple of calls, and a good retriever. For a large pond, an ideal setup would be a few dozen mixed big duck and teal decoys with one motorized flapping or feeding decoy. Use mallard feeding calls and teal whistlers sporadically, and certainly if you see ducks flying.

Deer hunters with a penchant for waterfowling should bring a shotgun, appropriate loads, and decoys to deer camp. They could get in on some bonus wing-shooting action.

River hunting is another good option in the region, as there is virtually no hunting pressure in some areas, and a fair number of wood ducks present. Wood ducks are surprisingly plentiful in some areas, and migrant ducks will hold up in low-lying wetlands along the river edge.

The problem with river hunting is some of the legalities involved. Most of the land along the rivers is privately owned, and some landowners think they own the riverbed as well—and in some cases, they do. Well, sort of.

A new law states that hunting is illegal over private land that is submerged for even part of the year. In most cases, hunting the middle of one of the shallow, thin rivers in the region would be all right. However, venturing onto the edge and setting up could be risky.

The new law reads that "a person may not hunt or take any wild animal or wild bird when the person is on or over privately owned land that is: submerged under public fresh water due to seasonal or occasional inundation."

That is a pretty broad interpretation, and something that could get would-be river hunters into trouble if they do not watch it.

Texans can hunt on most navigable stretches of river, although some areas like those that run through cities are off-limits. The best advice I can give you is to call a game warden in the area you plan to hunt and ask. That could save you a whole lot of trouble.

PUBLIC HUNTING HOTSPOTS

Area: Aguilla Wildlife Management Area

Location: Hill Country

Primary species: Mallard, widgeon, scaup, teal, ringneck

Hotspots: The north end of the lake where Hackberry Creek enters is good for puddle duck hunting. Divers are best on the more open water at the south end.

Special Regulations: Hunters must have an Annual Public

A good retriever is an invaluable asset no matter where you hunt in the Hill Country

Hunting Permit and be mindful of the duck sanctuary area.

Notes: When the pressure gets heavy here, the sanctuary area can make hunting quite difficult.

Contact: Texas Parks & Wildlife Department, 254-582-2719

Area: Granger Wildlife Management Area

Location: Williamson County

Primary species: Mallard, widgeon, ringneck, scaup, teal

Hotspots: The coves on the northern end of the lake usually provide the best overall hunting.

Special Regulations: Hunters must possess an Annual Public Hunting Permit.

Notes: Some of the units are closed periodically, so it is best to call ahead and check which areas are open.

Contact: U.S. Army Corps of Engineers, 512-859-2668

Area: Colorado River

Location: Numerous Hill Country counties

Primary species: Gadwall, teal, ringneck, wood duck, mallard

Hotspots: Some of the tributaries around Columbus are excellent. Another good location is in the northern reaches of the system in some of the open flats on the main body of the river.

Special Regulations: N/A

Notes: There is very little hunting pressure along this river system, so it's a great spot for hunters looking for some seclusion and for ducks seeking the same thing.

Contact: Texas Parks & Wildlife Department, 1-800-792-1112

Area: Guadalupe River

Location: Numerous Hill Country counties

Primary species: Gadwall, wood duck, mallard, teal, ringneck

Hotspots: Any area with little human presence will hold fair to good numbers of ducks in the winter.

Special Regulations: N/A

Notes: This is one of the most widely used recreational rivers in the state and receives a lot of fishing, tubing, and, in parts, boating pressure.

Contact: Texas Parks & Wildlife Department, 1-800-792-1112

Gadwall, like this one bagged by the "Duck Commander" Phil Robertson, can get thick along the eastern edge of Central Texas.

Area: Stillhouse Hollow Reservoir

Location: Bell County

Primary species: Gadwall, teal, mallard, widgeon, scaup, ringneck

Hotspots: The grassy shorelines on the south end of the lake provide some of the best hunting.

Special Regulations: Hunt in designated hunting areas and adjacent waters only. Hunters are allowed to use shot no larger than No. 2. Hunters can use only temporary blinds that must be removed at the end of each hunt. Hunters may not hunt within 600 feet of private property or within a designated recreation area.

Notes: This overlooked area can provide some excellent hunting, particularly just after a good cold front.

Contact: U.S. Army Corps of Engineers, 254- 939-2461

Area: Llano River

Location: Numerous Hill Country counties

Primary species: Gadwall, teal, mallard, wood duck, ringneck

Hotspots: Some of the bigger arms of the river north and south of Llano hold fair to good concentrations of ducks when the water is up.

Special Regulations: N/A

Notes: This is an incredibly scenic river with very little hunting pressure, so if you can find a good spot that is holding ducks, you have a strong shot at success.

Contact: Texas Parks & Wildlife Department, 1-800-792-1112

Chapter Seven

Waterfowl Hotspots:
South Texas Plains & Big Bend

The South Texas Plains and Big Bend regions not only run together geographically, but they have one very important element to waterfowl hunting in common: a general lack of water.

This arid part of the state does not appear as a classic waterfowling destination, but it does hold a surprising number of ducks, and this is probably due to very little hunting pressure. According to Texas Parks & Wildlife Department (TPWD) surveys, the South Texas Plains (which did not include several counties generally considered part of the region) produced only 2 percent of the ducks taken in Texas in the 2005 midwinter survey. That is in contrast to the region holding a whopping 15 percent of the ducks in that same year. When you take into consideration the fact there are no marshes or playa lakes, and very few reservoirs, that is an impressive percentage.

TPWD does no waterfowl surveys in the Big Bend region, but that does not mean it is barren of ducks. I have talked with hunters with deer leases in places like Ozona that report seeing large numbers of ducks on stock tanks and in creek beds with adequate water.

There are not many options for waterfowl hunters wishing to venture to the Big Bend, but there might be something that can draw your attention to the vast country.

Stock tanks in Southwest Texas can be loaded with ducks as this photo taken near Del Rio shows.

Cinnamon teal, which are rare just about everywhere in Texas, are killed in the Big Bend and along the southwestern edge of the South Texas Plains. These ducks are prized by hunters in Texas as a genuine trophy because of their sheer beauty as well as rarity.

"I got a deer lease west of Ozona, and was excited when I got on it because of the presence of mule deer, whitetails, and hybrids," said Justin Killian of San Antonio. "But when I was out bowhunting and saw a bunch of cinnamon teal on one of the ponds, I practically forgot about the deer and could not wait until duck season opened, and I was able to set up and get me a drake for the wall."

Killian said at times on his lease, he found all kinds of ducks and occasionally some geese: "We had planted some rye grass and one day saw a flock of snow geese and a few specklebelly on it. If I thought it was weird seeing ducks on the lease, you can imagine what I thought of the geese."

Bufflehead

Northern Shoveler

Greater Scaup

Northern Pintail

Mallard

Ring-Necked Duck

Blue-Winged Teal

Common Goldeneye

Wood Duck

Red-Breasted Merganser

Common Merganser

American Green-Winged Teal

C/4

American Wigeon

Gadwall

Hooded Merganser

Canvasback

Redhead

Ruddy Duck

Lesser Snow Goose

Canada Goose

Black Duck

DECOY PATTERNS

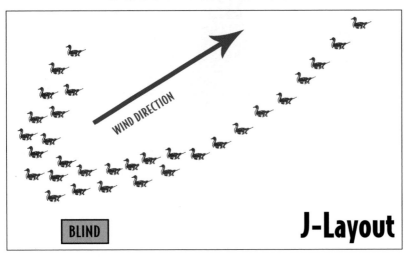

WIND DIRECTION

BLIND

J-Layout

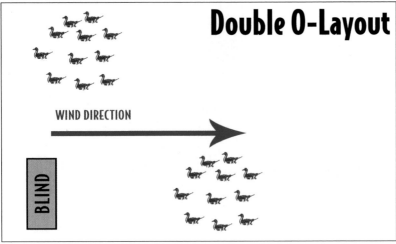

Double O-Layout

WIND DIRECTION

BLIND

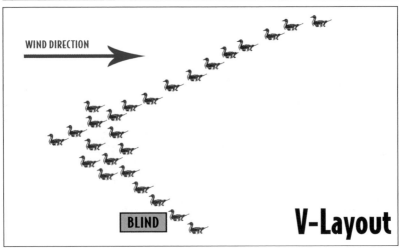

WIND DIRECTION

BLIND

V-Layout

As far as strategies for the region go, there are no real "go-to" techniques specifically for the area. However, there are some things to keep in mind.

For the reservoirs available here, the same strategies employed on other big-water areas work. Stick with big spreads when hunting divers, and medium-sized ones in the backwater for puddle ducks.

For river systems in the South Texas Plains, bring along a wood duck whistle call. You might be surprised to see how many wood ducks you can find along the wooded river bottoms of the Nueces and Sabinal River areas. The best part is that some of these woodies are Texas born and get very little pressure. I have always found calling wood ducks somewhat difficult, and that is probably because I hunt them in East Texas, where they get serious pressure. In un-pressured places, you can call them with surprising ease.

Spoonbill decoys are good choices for the Brush Country. The species shows up in fair to good numbers there. The white on the drakes is a good visual for ducks to key on.

For river and stock tank hunting, I recommend in both regions using very visible decoys. By "visible" I mean big and bright. Although the presence of pintails is spotty, I would go with a few pintail drake decoys and mix them up with teal, spoonbill drakes in full plumage, and mallard.

Definitely use mechanical decoys. In regions with light pressure, I have found that mechanicals work like a charm. At the time of this writing, I am corresponding with a landowner out near Alpine who says he has a lot of ducks on his property in the winter, and I am planning a trip. I plan to bring my Mojo, a feeding decoy, and a couple of dozen mixed teal, pintail, and spoonbills. If you have water in areas with little water during migrations, you will see lots of ducks, but on leases with a number of stock tanks, you want to draw attention to the one you are hunting. Ditto for stretches of river in the region.

Mechanical decoys can be a real help for hunters wanting to draw in ducks in the lightly pressured areas of the Trans-Pecos and Brush Country.

Hunters using retrieving dogs might want them to have them snake-proofed. This is something hunters usually do for quail dogs, but retrievers encounter plenty of snakes, too. Down here, water will draw in snakes like a magnet, and I am talking about big, dangerous snakes like western diamond-backs.

Something else to watch out for throughout south and west Texas is illegal immigrants. Hunters, including me, have encountered illegal aliens coming through the Mexican border for decades, but over the last five years or so, there has been an increasing amount of violence and drug trafficking in the area, and hunters are at risk. Part of this is that a lot of immigrants now are working directly for the drug trade in Central and South America, and they are frequently armed and dangerous. The risks are especially real for waterfowlers who venture into remote river drainages, which illegals use as travel ways.

If you encounter illegals, leave them alone and in most cases, they will leave you alone. If you are hunting, at least you will be armed if something happens, but you should probably consider going armed for self-protection even when you are scouting.

When coming across a spot that turns out to be a virtual highway for illegals, simply hunt somewhere else and call the border patrol. Even if the spot is loaded with ducks, it might not be worth a bad encounter.

PUBLIC HOTSPOTS

Area: James Daughtrey Wildlife Management Area (Choke Canyon Reservoir)

Location: Live Oak/McMullen Counties

Primary species: Teal, scaup, pintail, redhead, gadwall

Hotspots: Water levels here fluctuate greatly. When water levels are up, the backwaters can be excellent. Main lake points are good for divers.

Special Regulations: An Annual Public Hunting Permit is required for all hunters here. The management area is the land surrounding Choke Canyon Reservoir. All hunters must remain within 50 feet of the lake when hunting on days when the area is listed as closed.

Notes: This is probably the best inland public hunting in South Texas.

Contact: David Synatzske, 830-569-8700.

Area: Lake Corpus Christi

Location: Twenty miles northeast of Corpus Christi

Primary species: Teal, ringneck, scaup, redhead, pintail, gadwall

Hotspots: Reservoir levels fluctuate greatly here so conditions vary greatly from season to season. Diver hunting can be fantastic on the major points.

Special Regulations: A person may hunt ducks and geese during the open season with a shotgun in the portion of Lake Corpus Christi in San Patricio County. This exception does not apply to hunting within one mile of the Boy Scout camp, the Girl Scout camp, or Lake Corpus Christi Park. Officials list all other areas as a "wildlife sanctuary."

Notes: As is usual with any area like this that has a sanctuary, there tends to be lots of birds in the no-hunting zones.

Contact: Texas Parks & Wildlife Department, 1-800-792-1112.

Area: Lake Red Bluff

Location: Loving and Reeves Counties

Primary species: Teal (including cinnamon), bufflehead, widgeon

Hotspots: No specific hot spots are available for this seldom-hunted water body.

Special Regulations: Hunters are required to have a $40 annual public hunting permit.

Notes: This is a small body of water with little hunting pressure, but at times it can be loaded with ducks.

Contact: Red Bluff Water Control District, 432-445-2037.

Area: Lake Falcon

Location: On Mexican border in Zapata and Starr Counties

Primary species: Teal, Mexican whistler, shoveler, specklebelly

Hotspots: Big Tigers and School Bus areas

Shallow flats along the edge of the big reservoirs in the region can offer excellent hunting for well-concealed waterfowlers.

Special Regulations: Be careful not to cross over onto the Mexican side of the lake. You could find yourself in real trouble.

Notes: Big spreads of decoys and mechanical decoys will help you gain success here.

Contact: International Boundary & Water Commission, 956-848-5211.

Area: Lake Amistad

Location: Along the Mexican border in Val Verde County

Primary species: Teal (some cinnamon), Mexican whistler, fulvous tree duck, specklebelly, ringneck

Hotspots: The main lake points and coves in the Castle Canyon area offer some of the most consistent shooting.

Special Regulations: A permit fee of $20 is in effect here and the permit is available at the Amistad National Recreation Area headquarters. Failure to comply with federal hunting regulations will result in immediate cancellation of your hunting permit. Failure to return a completed Hunter Data Sheet showing hunt dates, hunt areas, game hunted, and game harvested could result in issuance of a $100 fine and you will not be allowed to hunt the following season.

Contact: National Park Service, Amistad Hunting Department, 830-775-7491, extension 206

Area: Nueces River

Location: Throughout South and Central Texas

Primary species: Wood ducks, merganser, teal, mallard, pintail, widgeon

Hotspots: Any area with good timber and shallow flats for ducks to feed in can provide good hunting.

Special Regulations: As with any river in this region, be mindful of not hunting on private property without permission. You can legally hunt riverbeds, but must not stray onto private property.

Notes: Wood duck hunting in parts of this river can be surprisingly good.

Contact: There are no available contacts for this river system.

Area: Sabinal River

Location: In the South-Central part of the state

Primary species: Mallards, gadwall, teal, merganser, wood duck, widgeon

Hotspots: No particular hot spots are available for this area.

Special Regulations: As with any river in this region, be mindful of not hunting on private property without permission. You can legally hunt riverbeds, but must not stray onto private property.

Notes: Easy access to the Sabinal River is difficult to find, but if you have a deer lease nearby, or access to property along more remote sections of river, it can harbor some good duck hunting.

Contact: There are no available contacts for this river system.

Area: Devil's River

Location: Big Bend/South Plains area of Texas

Primary species: Teal, gadwall, widgeon, pintail

Hotspots: Any area with shallow water for dabbling ducks to feed.

Special Regulations: As with any river in this region, be mindful

PHOTO COURTESY OF THE U.S. FISH AND WILDLIFE SERVICE

Cinnamon teal are a prized duck in Texas, and a species hunters in the Trans-Pecos are likely to encounter.

of not hunting on private property without permission. You can legally hunt riverbeds, but must not stray onto private property.

Notes: The hunting in this region can be feast or famine. The best hunting is around a strong cold front. Many of the ducks here do not hang around long and use it as a transitional point.

Contact: Texas River Bass Outfitters, 281-750-1343.

Area: Pecos River

Location: Big Bend region

Primary species: Teal (including cinnamon), bufflehead, widgeon, mallard

Hotspots: Any good area with shallow water for dabbling ducks to feed.

Special Regulations: As with any river in this region, be mindful of not hunting on private property without permission. You can legally hunt riverbeds, but must not stray onto private property.

Notes: Any ducks migrating through this region will likely stop on this river system. It is about the only water source for much of the region besides stock tanks.

Contact: There are no available contacts for this river system.

Chapter Eight

Waterfowl Hotspots:
Prairies and Lakes &
Panhandle Plains

Most hunters do not typically think of the northern third of Texas as a waterfowl hunting Mecca, but that is a mistake. During the 2005 midwinter survey, Texas Parks & Wildlife Department officials counted 13 percent of the duck population in the Panhandle Plains, 20 percent in the adjoining region around Abilene, and another 14 percent around the Dallas-Forth Worth region. That is 47 percent of the midwinter population!

Prairies and Lakes and the Panhandle Plains regions have some of the best hunting in the state. In this chapter, we will divide the information into the Panhandle (High Plains Mallard Management Unit), the North Zone, comprised of the areas along the Texas-Oklahoma border and Dallas-Forth Worth Metroplex, and finally, areas to the south.

Let's begin with the Panhandle. This region offers the best mallard hunting in the state with very little hunting pressure.

"I have been going out that way to hunt for the last few years, and you basically cannot find steel shot west of Fort Worth, so bring plenty with you if you plan a hunt out there. There are lots of ducks and, more importantly, lots of mallard," said guide Roger Bacon of Jasper.

Hunting is available on a few lakes in the region as well as a couple

The High Plains Mallard Management Area offers some of the best mallard hunting action in the state.

of wildlife management areas, but the bulk of the duck hunting is on playa lakes, which are small glacially-created lakes that dot the landscape by the thousands.

Access to some of these areas is limited, although a few outfitters offer hunting on them. There are still landowners that allow free hunting on their property for those who are polite enough to ask.

REGIONAL STRATEGIES

Decoy spreads for ducks in the region need not be huge or very fancy, as much of the hunting is on small water. On small waters, a couple of dozen decoys in conjunction with a mechanical decoy can get the mallard (and gadwall and other species) falling out of the sky.

"The pressure here is nothing compared to what it is on the coast, and the ducks act that way," said John Armstrong of Lubbock. "I'm not saying they are not wary, as all ducks are pretty wary, but they do not act like the ones that you come across on public areas on the coast."

Armstrong recommended that hunters traveling to the region not be afraid to hunt for mallard specifically: "If you come out to hunt for mallard, do not be afraid to pass on the gadwalls and the other ducks that come in. Sometimes, the mallard will fly a little later, so you if you want a bunch of greenheads, be patient."

Goose hunting in the region can be tremendous, particularly for Canadas, which are more abundant here than in any other region of the state. Just as with ducks, the geese here are not as pressured as they are in other areas, so the hunting can seem paradise-like for hunters who are used to

Goose hunting action in the Panhandle can be tremendous, with hunting access fairly easy to find.

crowded public areas on the coast.

"The goose hunting is good," Armstrong said. "Hunters should make sure to always keep plenty of Canada decoys in the spread, and be very mindful of movement while hunting. If they can stay still and put out a spread of a few hundred mixed shells, rags, kites, and full-body decoys, there is no reason you cannot score on geese here; that is, if you are hunting where they are feeding."

Geese are notorious for feeding heavily on one particular food source and then switching to another. It is best to talk with local farmers if you plan on going up to the region and asking which crops the birds are hitting heaviest. If they are hitting the crops, the farmers will gladly let you know and often let you hunt for a minimal fee or even free.

Hunters should use a variety of decoys to score on Panhandle geese.

In the North Zone area of the Prairies and Lakes region, hunters typically find different hunting conditions with far more pressure and many more restrictions related to development. This is chiefly a duck hunting area without much organized goose hunting activity.

The reservoirs in the region can offer some surprisingly good hunting, especially during the first few cold fronts of the season, when hunters here get a crack at migrating ducks before they reach the heavily hunted areas to the south. A big limiting factor on the quality of hunting on the reservoirs is drought. The region has been drought-plagued in recent years, which limits much of the hunting to the main body of the reservoirs.

Hunters utilizing large spreads and available cover on the main lakes can usually score on a mixed bag of ducks, including the highly sought-after mallard. Hunters with access to creeks, riverbeds, and the backwater of reservoirs with timber can find excellent mallard and wood duck shooting, much like that which is available in Arkansas.

A helpful hint for this area is to use mechanical decoys sparingly. If it seems the birds might be flaring from your mechanical, pull it. Many hunters use them in this region where outdoor superstores are seemingly on every corner. During the 2005-2006 seasons, I had numerous hunters tell me that after the first week of the season, their mechanicals seemed to do more harm than good. Bring them along and try them, but once they wear out their welcome, stick to the standard stuff.

Specklebelly are a bonus to hunters targeting ducks in the North Zone.

PUBLIC HUNTING HOTSPOTS

Area: Gene Howe Wildlife Management Area

Location: Near Canadian

Primary Species: mallard, widgeon, teal, scaup, ringneck, Canada geese

Hotspots: Only certain areas of the refuge are open.

Special Regulations: Hunters must possess an Annual Public Hunting Permit and register on-site.

Notes: Call ahead for open dates.

Contact: Texas Parks & Wildlife Department, 806-323-8642.

Area: Playa Lakes Wildlife Management Area (Taylor Lake Unit)

Location: Near Paducah

Primary Species: teal

Hotspots: The restored playa lake here is only 85 acres, so hotspots are generally where hunters can get to shoot.

Special Regulations: Hunters must possess an Annual Public Hunting Permit and register on-site.

Notes: At the time of this writing, the only duck hunting allowed was during the early teal season, and special draw hunts during the youth-only season.

Contact: Chip Ruthven, 806-492-3405

Area: Lake Texoma

Location: On the Texas-Oklahoma border north of Dallas

Primary Species: gadwall, teal, mallard, widgeon, scaup, ringneck

Hotspots: There are numerous hotspots on this huge body of water. Some of the backwater areas (when water levels are high) can provide some excellent mallard shooting.

Special Regulations: The Tishomingo Wildlife Refuge is located on the Oklahoma side of the lake and offers three hunt areas. Wildlife Management Unit (3 areas) is open for waterfowl hunting until noon on Tuesdays, Thursdays, Saturdays, and Sundays only. Waterfowl hunters are required to be off the unit by noon. No hunter check-station is operated. Blind or pond selection is on a first-come, first-served basis. Only waterfowl hunters may drive into the Check Station Unit. Sign-in and blind selection begins at 4:30 a.m. No entry before 5 a.m. is permitted. Hunters waiting for entry time are encouraged to coordinate with other hunters about which blind or pond they have chosen to hunt.

Teller Pond, Blind No. 14, and Blind No. 27 (Hog Pen Blind) are reserved for handicapped hunters who possess a non-ambulatory permit to hunt from a motorized vehicle issued by the ODWC. These hunters are authorized only to drive off road to gain access to these locations. If these three locations are not selected by a handicapped hunter by 5:30 a.m., they may be chosen by any hunter.

Decoy use is mandatory for waterfowl hunting. Boats and retrieving dogs are allowed. Dogs must remain under control of their handler.

There are also numerous wildlife management areas scattered throughout the lake. There is a 355-acre unit in the Burns Run Area, a 457-acre unit below Denison Dam; a 60-acre unit in the Willow Springs Area; a 150-acre unit in the Kansas Creek Area; a 100-acre unit on the north side of Alberta Creek; 110 acres in the Limestone Creek Area; a 250-acre unit on the Treasure Island, North Island Group; a 500-acre unit southwest of McLaughlin Creek; an 1100-acre unit in the Washita Point Area; a 1200-acre unit north of Newberry Creek; a 300-acre unit south of the Butcher Pen area; an 800-acre unit on either side of highway 70 east of the Roosevelt Bridge; a 1000-acre unit in the Lakeside area; and a 208-acre unit west of Plat. Only temporary blinds may be constructed and they must be removed at the end of each trip.

Notes: This lake can get very rough very quickly. Be mindful of safety when hunting on the main lake in particular.

Contact: U.S. Army Corps of Engineers, 202-761-0011; Tishomingo National Wildlife Refuge, 580-371-2402.

Area: Truscott Lake

Location: Near Crowell

Primary Species: mallard, pintail, teal scaup, ringneck, specklebelly

Hotspots: Main lake points can provide excellent shooting on the coming of cold fronts.

Special Regulations: Hunting at Truscott Lake is in accordance with applicable Federal and state regulations. Unless otherwise posted or as designated on maps, hunting is permitted in designated project hunting areas with archery and shotguns only. Generally, all Truscott Lake lands are open to the public for hunting, except developed recreational areas and lands around the dam and other structures.

Notes: Call in advance for water and hunting conditions.

Contact: U.S. Army Corps of Engineers, 940-474-3293

Area: Lake Meredith

Location: Near Fritch

Primary Species: mallard, pintail, wood duck, widgeon, scaup, canvasback

Hotspots: The best main lake hunting is on the south-central portion of the lake. The backwaters on the south end can provide strong shooting as well when water levels allow.

Special Regulations: No special permits are required.

Notes: This is an out of the way area for many hunters, but it does not receive much hunting pressure after the first split and can be excellent late in the season.

Contact: National Park Service, 806-857-3151.

Area: Possum Kingdom

Location: Near Graford

Primary Species: scaup, mallard, gadwall, wood duck, teal, red-head, widgeon

Hotspots: There is little information available about hunting here. Hunting is limited to designated blinds.

Special Regulations: Hunters must apply for a limited number of blinds available at $200 apiece.

Notes: If you want a blind, apply early. I called about this area in April and there was only one left, so hunters obviously book them up far in advance.

Contact: Brazos River Authority, 940-779-2321

Area: Grapevine Lake

Location: Near Grapevine in the Dallas-Forth Worth area

Primary Species: teal, gadwall, mallard, wood duck, scaup, canvasback

Hotspots: Hunting is limited to the Marshall Creek area.

Special Regulations: Permits for waterfowl are granted on a first-come, first-served basis, with a limit of 200 permits for the season.

Notes: This is another area where you need to get your permits quickly, as it is highly popular with Dallas-Forth Worth locals.

Contact: Grapevine Lake Project Office, 817-481-4541

Area: Lake Lewisville

Location: Lewisville

Primary Species: teal, gadwall, mallard, wood duck, scaup, canvasback

Hotspots: Hunting is greatly restricted due to the presence of homes, so hotspots are basically wherever hunting is allowed.

Special Regulations: A special permit is required to hunt here, available through the Lewisville Project Office. It is the hunter's responsibility to observe property lines and be aware of the boundaries of the hunting area. In addition, a 600-foot wide buffer strip beginning at the government property line and extending toward the lake is closed to hunting to ensure the safety of adjacent property owners. Hunting is restricted to the use of shotguns with shot no larger than No. 4.

Notes: Pay special attention to regulations here. This area is checked quite heavily by wardens, so be mindful of all details of the law.

Contact: Lewisville Project Office, 972-434-1666

Area: Lake Whitney

Location: North of Waco

Primary species: Mallard, widgeon, teal, scaup, ringneck

Hotspots: Main lake points

Special Regulations: Hunters should visit http://www.swf-wc.usace.army.mil/whitney/pages/hunting.htm to get a form that must be filled out before hunting. Hunters without access to the internet or first time hunters may register for a permit by sending a copy of the required documentation and a self-addressed stamped envelope to: Whitney Lake Office, 285 CR 3602, Clifton, TX 76634. You may register in person at the Whitney Lake Office at the west end of the dam on State Hwy 22 in Laguna Park, Monday through Friday from 8:00 a.m. to 4:30 p.m. All permitted hunters will receive a permit card and vehicle tag. Hunters must have this card on their person when hunting at Whitney Lake. Another regulation requirement is that hunters wear a minimum of 400 square inches of daylight fluorescent orange above the waist (at least 144 square inches must be visible on both the chest and back) and some type of orange headwear when walking in a designated hunting area. Persons hunting may remove the orange outerwear when they reach their blind or immediate hunting area.

Notes: Hunter surveys from the 2005 season showed a high level of success. Out of 13 duck hunters surveyed, they bagged 114 ducks over 42 days of hunting.

Contact: U.S. Army Corps of Engineers, 254-622-3332

Area: Brazos River

Location: Prairies and Lakes

Primary species: Wood duck, mallard, pintail, teal, ringneck

Hotspots: The better hunting is in the northern part of the system.

Special Regulations: N/A

Notes: Hunters that can locate wood duck roosting sites can get into some surprisingly good shooting by setting up in their flyway. This system in some areas has lots of wood ducks.

Contact: Texas Parks & Wildlife Department, 1-800-792-1112

Area: Lake Somerville Wildlife Management Area

Location: Near Ledbetter

Primary species: Gadwall, teal, mallard, wood duck

Hotspots: The hunting on the south end of the system seems to be the most consistent.

Special Regulations: Hunters must possess an Annual Public Hunting Permit.

Notes: The area has some beautiful bottomlands that when flooded can provide some excellent hunting.

Contact: Tim Bradle, 979-289-2392

Area: Lake Waco

Location: Near the city of Waco

Primary species: Gadwall, mallard, teal, scaup, wood duck, widgeon

Hotspots: Main lake points

Special Regulations: You must get a special form to hunt this body of water in most locations. You can find it online at http://www.swf-wc.usace.army.mil/waco/duck.htm. You can get one via mail at U.S. Army Corps of Engineers, ATTN: Hunting Coordinator, 3801 Zoo Park Drive, Waco, TX 76708

Notes: The mallard shooting here can be surprising in a good season.

Contact: U.S. Army Corps of Engineers Hunting Coordinator, 254-756-5359

Area: Lake Belton

Location: Near Killeen

Primary species: Gadwall, teal, mallard, widgeon, scaup, ringneck

Hotspots: The designated hunting area on the extreme north end is good, as is the one on the west side of White Flint Park.

Special Regulations: Hunt in designated hunting areas and adjacent waters only. Hunters are allowed to use no shot larger than No. 2. Hunters can use only temporary blinds that must be removed at the end of each hunt. Hunters may not hunt within 600 feet of private property or within a designated recreation area.

Contact: U.S. Army Corps of Engineers, 254-939-2461

Chapter Nine

Waterfowl Hotspots:
The Pineywoods

The Pineywoods of East Texas has always held a special place in my heart. Part of it is probably because I grew up jumping wood ducks off creeks in Jasper and Newton counties, but it mostly has to do with the fact that this area offers opportunities to hunt ducks in the timber and on big, open water.

Let's start with timber hunting and the most consistent and populous duck here: the wood duck.

The author awaits some low pass shooting at wood duck in a flooded slough in Newton County along the Sabine River near Burkeville.

Woodies are native birds, meaning they are born, live, breed, and die in the Pineywoods region for the most part. There are migrant wood duck as well, but most are Texas born and end up Texas dead if you have a good hunt.

Wood duck love to hang out in flooded timber, where they forage for acorns and other goodies. Watching them fly in and out of the canopy is truly amazing. They are such acrobats that sometimes you almost forget to shoot at them.

I once had the good fortune of seeing several thousand wood duck fly to roost on some private property in Newton County. I will never forget seeing a couple cross over this line of pines, and then a few dozen, then a few hundred, and then the sky was black with whistling wood duck. It was a truly remarkable sight.

Hunters wanting to score on wood duck need to do some scouting and figure where they are flying. Woodies will light in a small decoy spread, but mostly you have to be right on where they want to feed or along their flight path.

A good wood duck whistle call is a necessity if you want to try to lure them into shooting range, assuming they are not flying where you want them to be. They are certainly not the most responsive duck to calls, but someone who can really do a good woody whistle usually gets their two-bird limit. You have to keep in mind that many of the woodies are natives and know their areas better than migrant ducks. Anything that looks out of place will red flag them.

Mallard and gadwall also frequent the flooded timber, and hunters that locate open areas within the timber and set up a good decoy spread along with an automated decoy, like a Mojo duck, can score big.

"Moving decoys are really good in the timber in the Pineywoods," said my hunter-cousin, Frank Moore. It is not like hunting out on the open water or prairie, where ducks can see everything. Looking from the sky down through the trees; they have a limited view, so a motion decoy is important. It would be a good idea to have one with moving wings, and some feeders down as well."

Moore is also a big believer in having decoys that the ducks can see: "I'm all into mixing quite a few magnums in with the standard decoys. It is all about making a good visual impression. The ducks have to see you before they have a reason to commit."

Calling is also important, as it can be the key turning point for ducks not exactly sold on the decoys.

"If you have mallard and gadwall around, call, call, and call again," Moore said. "You can bring both in fairly easily if you are using motion decoys. Have a good facemask or paint on, and good camouflage that matches your surroundings. Gadwall in particular will light like crazy if you can speak the language using this strategy."

On the other end of the spectrum is the open water hunting on the

Capt. Skip James tries to turn some mallard headed toward a slough just past his decoy spread.

many reservoirs in the region. Roger Bacon guides on Rayburn and Steinhagen, and said many hunters just do not realize how much quality hunting is on the lakes they fish for bass, crappie, and catfish ever year: "We have some amazing duck hunting at times, and the best part is, we have a large population of one of the most prized ducks in the country—canvasbacks. Between Rayburn and Toledo Bend in particular, we hold a large number of canvasbacks that can give hunters something they might've thought they could never get in such large numbers."

While hunting with Bacon in early 2006, I had several instances of more than 50 canvasbacks all locked up and ready to light in the decoys. I am simply a fanatic about these birds, so it was really thrilling for me.

This sequence shot shows some canvasbacks coming in toward decoys on Sam Rayburn reservoir, one getting shot and hitting the water.

"To hunt canvasbacks or any of the divers, you have to have a pretty big spread and a believable one," Bacon said. Realistic color, shape, and the way they move on the water is important. Divers have a lot more options of where to go and what to eat than puddle ducks do in many instances, so to get them to come and hang around long enough to shoot, strict attention to detail is important."

While many hunters dislike having a lot of anglers on the water, Bacon said it could actually help duck hunters on the big lakes: "As long as the fishermen are not on top of you, they can help out. The divers will raft up in large concentrations, and boats moving around the lake will bust them up and disperse them in your direction if you're lucky."

PUBLIC HUNTING HOTSPOTS

Area: Toledo Bend Reservoir

Location: Along the Texas-Louisiana border in Newton and Sabine counties

Primary species: wood duck, canvasback, scaup, ringneck, teal

Hotspots: The Indian Mounds area is a great locale, as is the extreme northern end of the lake, especially when the water is high.

Special Regulations: Be mindful of shooting canvasbacks when in season, the limit is one, and many times they are legal game for only part of the season. Also, half of this lake is owned by Texas and the other half by Louisiana. Stick to hunting the Texas side of the lake.

Notes: If there is a drought, forget hunting puddle ducks. The diver hunting will be far better.

Contact: Greg Crafts, 409-368-7151

Area: Lake O' the Pines

Location: Near Jefferson

Primary species: wood duck, mallard, teal, scaup

Hotspots: Backwaters when they are flooded

Special Regulations: N/A

Notes: You do not hear much about the duck hunting here, but it can be quite productive.

Contact: Greenhead Guide Service, 903-797-2945

Area: Lake Livingston

Location: Polk County

Primary species: scaup, wood duck, teal, gadwall, mallard

Hotspots: The north end of the lake where the Trinity feeds into the main lake, and all of the tributaries in that section

Special Regulations: N/A

Notes: If you can manage to set up on the main body of the lake in a sink box or a well-camouflaged blind, you should get lots of action when the ducks are there.

Contact: Dave Cox, 936-291-9602

Area: Sam Rayburn Reservoir

Location: North of Jasper

Primary species: wood duck, gadwall, canvasbacks, scaup, teal

Hotspots: Top hunting spots here vary greatly. The coves north of the Powell Park area can be very good.

Special Regulations: N/A

Notes: The best hunting here is when there are many anglers moving around on the main lake to push around the big wads of divers.

Contact: Roger Bacon, 409-489-0444

Area: Lake Fork

Location: Near Emory

Primary species: wood duck, mallard, gadwall, teal, canvasback

Hotspots: Hunters that set up on the main body of the lake can get lots of action, as many of the shorelines are off limits due to development, making available shoreline crowded at times.

Special Regulations: N/A

Notes: This place has surprisingly good duck hunting and at times is one of the best in the region.

Contact: Lance Vick, 903-312-0609

Guide Roger Bacon shows off a rare redhead he took while hunting on Sam Rayburn reservoir.

Area: Tony Houseman State Park and Blue Elbow Wildlife Management Area

Location: Orange County

Primary species: wood duck, hooded merganser, mallard

Hotspots: The first two winding logging cuts of this area have numerous cuts intersecting them that lead to backwater. Try those spots.

Special Regulations: An Annual Public Hunting Permit is required to hunt here. Make sure you stick to the Texas side of the river. Louisiana is just a stone's throw away and the game wardens there do not appreciate out-of-state hunters that are not properly licensed.

Notes: This area is quite literally on the southern tip of the Pineywoods region. In fact, the part of this unit located south of Interstate 10, which is off limits to hunting, is where coastal marsh country begins. With that said, there are many gators here, so in the early season, be careful with your dogs. There are also lots of feral hogs to watch out for.

Contact: Jim Sutherlin, 409-736-2551

Area: B.A. Steinhagen Reservoir

Location: Near Jasper

Primary species: wood duck, canvasback, teal, mallard

Hotspots: Main lake flats on the southwest side of the lake

Special Regulations: Much of the reservoir on the north end of the lake is part of the Steinhagen Wildlife Management Area. On the south end, however, most of the land is open to hunting without an Annual Public Hunting permit.

Notes: The water levels fluctuate greatly here, so calling ahead and checking on conditions is recommended.

Contact: Gary Calkins, 409-389-6894

Area: Big Lake Bottom Wildlife Management Area

Location: Near Palestine

Primary Species: wood duck, gadwall, mallard

Hotspots: There are too many to list here. Most of the hunting is in the flooded bottoms, with fluctuating water levels being a key component to choosing a good spot.

Special Regulations: Hunter must possess an Annual Public Hunting permit to access the area. Dogs are illegal, except each permit holder may possess one dog while hunting waterfowl.

Notes: Hunting is usually open only part of the season here. Contact TPWD for more information.

Contact: Corey Mason, 903-389-7080

Area: Gus Engeling Wildlife Management Area

Location: Anderson County

Primary species: wood duck, mallard, gadwall

Hotspots: Open spots in the flooded timber

Special Regulations: All users must perform on-site registration daily and possess an Annual Public Hunting permit.

Notes: Be prepared for tough walking in the sloughs.

Contact: Hayden Haucke, 903-928-2251

Area: Cooper Wildlife Management Area

Location: Hopkins and Delta counties

Primary species: wood duck, teal, mallard, ringneck

Hotspots: Coves around the Lost Ridge area

Special Regulations: On-site registration is required for all hunts, and all hunters must possess a registration form while hunting. Hunters cannot leave decoys out over night.

Notes: This is another area loaded with wild hogs. Be careful when traversing the sloughs before daybreak.

Contact: Texas Parks & Wildlife Department, 903-945-3132.

Area: Richland Creek Wildlife Management Area

Location: Navarro and Freestone counties

Primary species: wood duck, mallard, teal, pintail

Hotspots: Lindsey Slough

Blake Fischer of Winnie ends a Pineywoods hunt on a good note with a mixed bag of canvasback and shoveler.

and Pea Patch Lake areas

Special Regulations: On-site self-registration is required for all visitors, including hunters. An Annual Public Hunting permit is required.

Notes: This area can be good during the late season, when some of the surrounding reservoirs start to turn off.

Contact: Jeffrey Gunnels, 903-389-7080

Area: Houston County Public Hunt Units 116 and 117

Location: Houston County

Primary species: wood duck, mallard, gadwall

Hotspots: No particular spots to speak of

Special Regulations: An Annual Public Hunting permit is required.

Notes: This is one of those areas you are going to have to do some scouting to locate good hunting spots.

Contact: Texas Parks & Wildlife Department, 800-792-1112

Area: Tawakoni Wildlife Management Area

Location: Houston and Tawakoni counties

Primary species: wood duck, mallard, gadwall, teal, scaup

Hotspots: North fork of the lake

Special Regulations: Hunting is restricted to the surface of Lake Tawakoni and within 100 feet of the existing water's edge. Waterfowl are the only legal species hunters may pursue. Waterfowl hunting is illegal within 300 yards of an inhabitable structure and within 100 yards of park boundaries, the dam, spillway, and SRA office area. An Annual Public Hunting permit is required.

Notes: When conditions are dry around the lake, the hunting is tough. If it is a wet winter, the hunting is usually tremendous.

Contact: Shaun Crook, 903-881-8233

Area: Angelina/Dam B Wildlife Management Area

Location: Jasper and Tyler counties

Primary species: wood duck, canvasback, teal, shoveler

Hotspots: For divers, target the main body of the lake, which makes up a large portion of this area. For wood duck and mallard, find the flooded flats accessible by the slews feeding the lake.

Special Regulations: Hunters must possess an Annual Public Hunting permit. Those who want to camp on the area must get a permit from the U.S. Army Corps of Engineers (409-429-3491).

Notes: If you hunt during the early teal season, be very cautious of alligators. The lake has a strong gator population and lots of very big specimens.

Contact: Gary Calkins, 409-384-6894

Area: Pat Mayse Wildlife Management Area

Location: Lamar County

Primary species: wood duck, mallard, teal

Hotspots: The Craddock Creek system

Special Regulations: All hunters must register on-site. Annual Public Hunting permits are required.

Notes: This can be a top-notch wood duck shot.

Contact: Jack Jernigan, 903-982-7107

Area: Caddo Lake Wildlife Management Area

Shallow-driving outboards like the Pro-Drive pictured here are crucial to hunting on parts of the Angelina/Dam B Wildlife Management Area.

Location: Harrison and Marion counties

Primary species: wood duck, mallard, gadwall, teal

Hotspots: Main lake islands

Special Regulations: An Annual Public Hunting permit is required.

Notes: This is one of those places that is so beautiful, it does not matter if you do not kill any ducks. Caddo is the largest and only natural lake in the state, and gets quite a bit of duck hunting pressure. If any place in Texas looks like a duck hotspot, it is Caddo.

Contact: Vanessa Adams, 903-679-9393

Area: White Oak Creek Wildlife Management Area

Location: Titus, Bowie, and Cass counties

Primary species: wood duck, mallard

Hotspots: Around White Oak Creek

Special Regulations: On-site registration is required. Hunters must possess a registration form while in the area. Hunters cannot leave decoys out overnight.

Notes: This is another truly beautiful area with killer scenery and sometimes-strong duck hunting.

Contact: John Jones, 903-884-3800

Area: Alazan Bayou Wildlife Management Area

Location: Nacogdoches County

Primary species: wood duck, mallard, gadwall

Hotspots: There is a section abutting the Angelina National Forest that is not open to hunting. This spot can be good for getting ducks pressured from other areas of the lake.

Special Regulations: On-site registration is required. Hunters must possess an Annual Public Hunting permit.

Mallard are thick in parts of the Pineywoods when there is plenty of water in the sloughs and backwater flats. When the region is dry, finding these prized ducks can be tough.

Notes: Be careful not to accidentally slip into the no-hunting portion of the National Forest next door. It might be tempting, but it is not worth it.

Contact: Joel Casto, 936-639-1879

Area: Newton County Public Hunt Unit 122

Location: Newton County

Primary species: wood duck

Hotspots: No specific hotspots known for this area

Special Regulations: Hunters must possess an Annual Public Hunting permit.

Notes: Hunters wanting to get a good crack at wood duck in an unpressured area might want to try this. Be careful, though—there are lots of deer hunters.

Contact: Gary Calkins, 409-384-6894

Area: Newton/Jasper County Public Hunt Unit 125

Location: Newton and Jasper counties

Primary species: wood duck

Hotspots: No specific hotspots for this area

Special Regulations: Hunters must possess an Annual Public Hunting permit.

Notes: There is good potential for wood duck. Beware of deer hunters with long-range rifles and of feral hogs.

Contact: Gary Calkins, 409-384-6894

Area: Newton/Jasper County Public Hunt Unit 144

Location: Newton and Jasper Counties

Primary species: wood duck

Hotspots: No specific hotspots

Special Regulations: Hunters must possess an Annual Public Hunting permit.

Notes: Another good wood duck locale.

Contact: Gary Calkins, 409-384-6894

Area: Panola County Public Hunt Unit 630

Location: Panola County

Primary species: wood duck, merganser, gadwall

Hotspots: No specific hotspots

Special Regulations: Hunters must possess an Annual Public Hunting permit.

Notes: There is little pressure here during the last season split.

Contact: Texas Parks & Wildlife Department, 800-792-1112

Area: Panola County Public Hunt Unit 607

Location: Panola County

Primary species: wood duck, mallard, merganser

Hotspots: No specific hotspots

Special Regulations: Hunters must possess an Annual Public Hunting permit.

Notes: There is little pressure here in the late season.

Contact: Texas Parks & Wildlife Department, 800-792-1112

Area: San Augustine County Public Hunt Unit 106

Location: San Augustine County

Primary species: wood duck, mallard, merganser

Hotspots: No specific hotspots

Special Regulations: Hunters must possess an Annual Public Hunting permit.

Notes: This is a popular spot with deer hunters, so be cautious moving around in this area.

Contact: Texas Parks & Wildlife Department, 800-792-1112

Area: North Toledo Bend Wildlife Management Area

Location: Shelby County

Primary species: wood duck, canvasback, scaup, mallard

Hotspots: Main lake points

Special Regulations: Onsite registration is required. Hunters must possess an Annual Public Hunting permit.

Notes: This is a place you might be able to bag a wood duck and a canvasback in the same spread.

Contact: Joel Casto, 936-639-1879

Area: Old Sabine Bottom Wildlife Management Area

Wood duck are the staple of the Pineywoods, and a more beautiful and tasty staple would be difficult to find.

Location: Smith County

Primary species: wood duck, mallard, teal

Hotspots: The northern boundary of the area along the river

Special Regulations: On-site registration is required. Hunters must possess an Annual Public Hunting permit. Parking is restricted to designated parking areas.

Notes: Due to the nature of the area, officials might close it down when there have been heavy rains, causing rapidly rising water that could be dangerous.

Contact: Shaun Crook, 903-881-8233

DO YOU NEED A GUIDE?

Waterfowl guides are an invaluable asset for hunters, particularly those without a boat. Guides have access to key hunting properties and the means to get there. If you hunt the Upper Coast, you are likely to be taken to your blind (and usually comfortable ones) in a mud boat, whereas on the Middle and Lower Coasts expect an airboat ride. In other parts of Texas, you might access an area via johnboat or on a four-wheeler.

Guides also provide decoys and retrievers, and are in most circumstances skilled- to expert-level callers. They are a great option for novice hunters who wish to learn more about the art of waterfowling, and can simply be a stress free way for veteran hunters to spend their time. They are also great for hunters who have little disposable time and cannot maintain a lease.

Hiring a guide is another issue altogether. There are many guides out there, and not all of them are good ones.

When looking for a guide, ask around or look on the internet message boards dedicated to waterfowling. Word of mouth is usually the best way to go when looking for a guided hunt.

Most of the time, recommendations will be for established services, and these are usually the best option. A long history in the business usually means that they are reputable and very good at what they do. When contacting a guide service, always ask for references. If they cannot provide you with phone numbers of past clients, avoid them like a kid avoids a bath. No references equals bad reputation.

When planning a hunt, make sure and tell the outfitter of any physical disabilities you might have, and other special needs. Communication is very important. A guide cannot make something happen for you if you do not ask for it.

Chapter Ten

Calling & Decoys

Two of the primary components of waterfowl hunting are calls and decoys. The two go hand in hand as crucial elements of allowing waterfowlers to fool their quarry into shooting range, and they add an artistic touch to the sport that other types of hunting simply do not have.

Let's examine calls and calling first.

Noted waterfowler John Taylor wrote that when it comes to selecting a call: "Today's duck hunter is confronted with a bewildering array of calls made of synthetic and wood, and single and double reeds.

"Wood calls tend to be softer in tone, and because wood absorbs moisture, they can change pitch as they expand and contract. Synthetics, mainly made of acrylic resin, don't change dimensions, and tend to be louder, although that's not always true.

"The biggest quandary is whether to pick a single or double reed. Single-reed calls are traditional, and are the exclusive choice of contest callers. Hunters will often find a double-reed call more appealing because they tend to have a more raspy sound that's closer to the sound of a hen mallard.

"The biggest mistake made is thinking that a double-reed call will compensate for improper calling style. Either way, single or double, you still have to blow the call correctly or it still sounds like a New Year's Eve party favor. The best advice is to try both and see which complements your calling style."

For beginners, I would recommend a double reed call because they are easier to use and a bit more consistent. Experienced hunters would do better to use a single reed call, as they tend to make sounds that are more realistic. One of the biggest mistakes made with novice callers is the idea that you "blow" into a call. You do not really blow at call; you "talk" into it. When

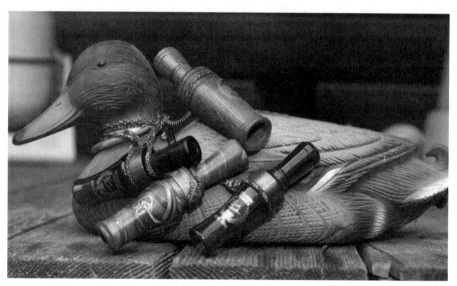

Lanyards are important for organizing calls and keeping things from getting cluttered in the duck blind.

you read instructions to say "tuk tuk tuk tuk tuk" or "tikit-tikit-tikit" into a call, they really mean to say it, or at least sort of groan it into the call.

Master caller and call maker Buck Gardner said there are many theories about duck calling, and he is not sure that any one of them works 100 percent of the time: "Sometimes ducks seem to want a lot of calling, with long and nearly continuous highballs. 'Put them on a string and don't give them time to think,' as the old reelfoot-style callers used to say.

"At other times and places, too much calling seems to put ducks off. Maybe not flaring them, but keeping them endlessly circling when they should be landing. Heavy hunting and calling pressure often results in call-shy birds, but sometimes I think it's a matter of their mood or some other factor that we don't understand. I favor the style of calling that puts ducks in the bag. I don't hesitate to change my style—more or less, loud or soft—when whatever I am presently doing isn't doing the job. Sometimes, a simple change-up from the locally popular calling style tells the birds something that they haven't already heard."

Gardner said he didn't win any of his duck-calling championships by showing up with no practice and otherwise unprepared to compete: "Neither do I go to the blind unready to do my best calling job to waterfowl. Neither should you. If you get a new call, it is a very wise idea to get the instructional tape or video that goes with it. Calls from different makers often blow a bit differently. Listening to the guy who made the call tell you how to blow it best is a far shorter learning curve than trial and error."

In terms of specific call sounds, there are all kinds of variations, but a handful are true standards. Ducks Unlimited (DU) put together a list of the best, and the ones their expert consultants consider essential to learn. Here it is, according to DU:

Greeting Call: "I use the greeting call when I first see ducks at a distance. It's a series of 5 to 7 notes in descending order at a steady even rhythm—*kanc, kanc, kanc, kanc, kanc*," said Rod Haydel, part of Louisiana duck calling royalty—the Haydel family of Haydel's Game Calls.

Feeding Call: For a basic feeding call, say "tikki-tukka-tikka" into the call, raising and lowering the volume slightly. "I don't feed call a lot," said three-time World Champion caller and call maker Mike McLemore. "Callers should learn to use it to add variety, but it sounds better to the caller than it does to the ducks." Haydel added: "Most mallards I hear feed-calling in the typical *kitty, kitty, kitty* fashion are flying, while ducks feeding are more broken up and erratic sounding, like *da-dit da-dit dit dit, da-dit dit.*"

Hail Call: The hail or highball call is an overused call in the minds of the pros. "Don't use a highball within 100 yards of the ducks," said Jim Olt of P.S. Olt Company. "But when you do use it, blow high, hard, and loud. However, nobody should use it unless they know how and when. Hails are the loudest of the lot." Rod Haydel agreed: "I'm not much on 30-note hail calls. I have yet to hear a real hen call in this manner. I try to sound as natural as I can." If you decide to try your hail call, start with a long, strong, *aaaaaink...aaaaaink... aaaaink, aaainkaink* and taper off as it progresses. Remember to use the hail call sparingly, and as Haydel said: "If the ducks are coming in, forget calling."

Comeback Call: "The comeback call is used when ducks don't respond to your greeting or you want an immediate response, such as in timber," Haydel said. "It's more urgent sounding and faster, like *kanckanc, kanc, kanc, kanc.* Also, I have found live hens only call to others after they have flown over the pond or passed their location. Usually she'll give them only one comeback call." Olt added: "Just remember that a comeback call is fast and hard, with about 5 to 7 notes. Don't overcomplicate it."

Lonesome Hen: The lonesome hen is an often-overlooked call that can be very effective, especially when ducks are call-shy. The call is nothing more than widely spaced, irregular, nasal, drawn-out *quaaaaink* quacks. Some callers have used it to pull birds sitting on the water for long distances. "You can derive your lonesome hen call from your basic quack. Learn to quack correctly, and the rest will come from that," Olt said. "Your lonesome call should be spaced out and quick, with several seconds between. If the quacks are too close together, it scares the ducks. And keep in mind that the lonesome hen is somewhat low and throaty."

Pleading Call: "The pleading or begging hail call is used to get the attention of ducks flying 75 to 200 yards above you," said champion caller Greg Brinkley. "This call is a series of 5 to 6 quacks that are really dragged out to sound like you are begging the ducks to land. A pleading call is a *kaaanc, kanc, kanc, kanc* sound, and its first note is usually held a little longer. The pleading call is a drawn-out, slightly faster variation of the come-back. Many callers save the pleading call for stubborn ducks that refuse to come in. It's the caller's way of literally pleading with the ducks to come into or return to the spread.

This mechanical mallard, in this case a Mojo, worked wonders for the author on a hunt in Sam Rayburn reservoir with guide Roger Bacon. Mechanicals work great when set up between two clusters of decoys.

Whistling (mallard, pintail, teal, wood duck, widgeon): Whistling works! Rod Haydel swears by a whistle: "Most of our most successful hunts last year were late in the season using whistles in conjunction with our mallard calls. We try to identify the ducks before we call to them so that we can speak their language."

I am personally a big fan of whistles. In the public marsh where I do a lot of hunting, most callers go overboard with their calling, and I have found a few toots of a whistle often turns ducks better than the other calls when the pressure is really on.

Now let's examine decoys, starting with the basic types:

Floaters: These are your basic floating duck or goose decoys that, as the name implies, float. A cord and small anchor keep them in place. Some have a built-in keel weight to help them float upright, while others do not.

Rags: Goose hunters use white or sometimes black rags or sheets of plastic spread across a field to entice geese.

Shells: These are typically goose decoys that have a realistic head but just a shell of a body.

Mangum: These are oversized decoys designed to draw birds from up high (waterfowl have poor depth perception). Magnums can range from mallard decoys twice the normal size to Canada goose decoys that literally double as a blind.

Life-size: The term "life-size" typically refers to full body, realistic goose decoys.

Mechanical: These are decoys with moving parts. Some simply have wings that move in the wind, while others are battery powered. A few models swim in circles or produce bubbles.

Kite: These are simply kites shaped like ducks or geese that are used when the wind is blowing strongly.

Two-Liter Soda Bottles: Two-liter plastic soda bottles can make decent decoys with the proper application of paint and a little imagination.

With an understanding of the kinds of decoys available, let's look at a few of my favorite spread patterns for different situations.

Snow geese: Think big in most applications with snow geese. Some guides use upward of 1500 decoys to lure these super wary, gregarious birds. My favorite setup is a basic "C" pattern with 700-1000 mixed decoys. Hunters who set up realistic spreads that show geese doing a variety of things will do much better than hunters with just a bunch of rags out in a field. The most realistic decoys should be on the downwind edge, where the geese will see them first on their final approach. The old adage in Texas used to be that you could draw snows with a white bucket in a field. That might have been true in the past, but not anymore. The species has developed a level of hunter awareness second to none in the waterfowl world.

Mix up your decoy spread with life-size, photo-realistic decoys, shells, rags, and kites. In recent years, I have seen kites popping up more and more at goose hunts, and believe they are one of the major keys to success, assuming the wind is with you. In December 2005, I got to participate in a hunt for Ducks Unlimited television, and our quarry was snow geese. We had lots of competition, as there were numerous highly skilled outfitters operating in the area. Our spread consisted of several strategically placed kites lined up within good shooting range of the hunters. Nearly every goose we shot went right for the kites.

Another set I like that is commonly used in northern states is the "wings" formation, which consists of one big mass of regular-sized decoys with two thin strips of magnums coming off the side. This is done by setting four or five decoys out in a cluster and making 20 or more groups like this. Spread the decoys out in a 150- to 200-yard area to create the natural appearance of how birds behave on clear days.

When goose hunting, it is important to be camouflaged head to toe, including a solid facemask. By the time geese get down to Texas, they have been shot at hundreds of times. Just as important to keep in mind is that snow geese in particular are an old population. The age-class of the birds is such that we are dealing with experts in dodging hunters. If you think you are not camouflaged enough, you are not.

Big-water ducks: Just like with snow goose hunting, the secret is to think big on open water, whether it is on the bay or on a reservoir. You want to set up a good number of duck decoys, particularly divers, which are common in the area this time of year, mixed with a few snow geese to get the bird's attention. Besides making the spread big, use big magnum-sized decoys. Besides mimicking nature, you have to focus the birds on your spread in open water, and using big decoys is a way to do that. When the birds are flying over open water, which is often choppy, they might have a hard time seeing regular-sized decoys or a small spread.

Many hunters set their decoys in a large cove, leave a landing area, and extend one or two long legs of the spread out into open water to attract cruising ducks (J and V layouts). This is highly effective, especially if you have in your spread a couple of mechanical duck decoys with rotating wings.

I prefer hunting around islands. The prime decoy spot is toward the tail of an island, in the soft water between the tail and the main current. Islands generally have enough cover that, coupled with a well-camouflaged boat, will work to hide hunters. Usually the best shooting time comes as the birds cross the bay after their morning feed in the marsh and nearby prairies. The J-layout is a good pattern to employ. *(see page C/8)* This consists of decoys set up in the shape of a "J" with the hunters set up in the middle or to one side of the spread. You can camouflage the boat and set up in the middle of the set, or hunt just off the edges on nearby land. With the end tapering off, it looks like a natural landing, inviting more birds to settle down.

Puddle ducks: A popular and effective puddle duck setup is called the "Double-O." *(see page C/8)* This is a very simple setup made of two round groups of decoys with a gap in the middle for ducks to land in. Remember, ducks and geese always land into the wind, so you will want to set up so that the birds will quarter toward your blind. With this spread, at least four dozen dekes are best.

River ducks: River hunting is sort of a lost art in Texas, but since I live right on the Sabine, it is something I have become quite fond of. When I hunt the rivers, I tend to go with a couple of dozen decoys and rely on motion instead of mass to attract the birds. I use a similar pattern to the puddle duck setup with the "Double O," but use a mechanical mallard in the middle set out about 20 yards, and have a swimming decoy to one side.

Ducks in the timber: Decoys in the timber are a whole different thing than anywhere else. Because of the obstructed view, you do not necessarily need a lot of decoys. A couple of dozen will do. Motion is something I find important to get the attention of fast-flying wood duck, mallard, and gadwall. A mechanical decoy is a good idea, as is the use of hooded merganser decoys. There are lots of mergansers in the timber in East Texas, and using a drake of the hooded variety will help draw in ducks, as the contrasting color pattern is easy to see from up high.

Ideally, you will have a big hole in the timber into which to attract ducks. If so, spread the

This modification of a kite decoy allows the hunter to position it on a pole. With no wind it leaves a decoy in the air and with wind the wings flap giving a truly lifelike appearance.

decoys along the edge of the hole and leave a landing spot in the middle.

Pass shooting geese: Sometimes, the best goose hunting involves no decoys at all. The main ingredient for success is fog. This is a trend I first noticed a few years ago while conducting waterfowl hunting reports for the *Port Arthur News*. It seemed every time thick sea fogs crept ashore, hunters reported excellent goose hunting action. This is almost exclusively a proposition of pass shooting the geese as they fly low, confused in the thick, misty blanket. The key is targeting the levees and ridges in the refuge system that low-flying geese use as roadways as they slowly cruise, heading to and from feeding areas. This is a time for hunters to employ calling once the geese get close, so they can lure them even closer for a shot. The best advice would be to use the call sparingly and to be prepared for the birds to be there a lot quicker than you might think.

Capt. Ryan Warhola of Port Acres, Texas, has had good success in bagging these low-flying geese, and emphasized that hunters need to be very mindful of weather conditions: "You have to really pay attention to the weather and be prepared to leave at the last minute because this is a matter of keying in on confused geese, and that's something you don't get a chance to do every day."

Warhola recommended that hunters get familiar with the flight patterns of the birds in the section of the refuge they want to hunt: "These birds have patterns they use quite a bit in different areas. They will do the same thing on foggy mornings, but they are not sure of their surroundings, so they are a lot easier to get. Find some good cover, like around a levee or just behind a small ridge, and use that as your signpost for shooting and calling. Once the birds get to your spot, let them have it. If the fog is high enough you can see a fair way up, you'll want to take farther shots, but if it's really thick, you can make super high-percentage shots at near point blank range."

DECOYING TIPS

- Use mechanical decoys sparingly. If it seems the birds might be flaring from your mechanical, pull it. Many hunters use them in this region, where outdoor superstores are seemingly on every corner. During the 2005-2006 seasons, I had numerous hunters tell me that after the first week of the season, their mechanicals seemed to do more harm than good. Bring them along and try them, but once they wear out their welcome, stick to the standard decoy setups.

- Hunters should be mindful of any reservoir that has been dry in recent years, but fills up this season. Drought does allow for vegetation growth that can be beneficial to waterfowl after it gets covered with water. Setting up decoys in a true vegetation rich area will score you more birds than trying to fake it over a sub-par feeding zone.

- On the coastal prairies, the best hunting is not necessarily when you might expect it. "We much prefer days with lots of sunshine," said outfitter Brian Fischer of Drake Plantation Outfitters. "I know that many people think of duck and goose hunting being best in terrible weather, but if we have a good wind and clear skies, they decoy much better around here. When you have high clouds, the hunting is tough. If you only have limited days to choose, pick a clear one, or if you want ducks in the prairie or marsh, rain is good because it gets them moving. Again, high, cloudy days are tough."

- Sometimes, early on the size of the decoy spread does not matter that much, but it is important to vary them up and have some pintails in the mix. "Pintails are light-colored and they are a duck we have a lot of," said avid waterfowler Frank Moore. "They tend to get the attention of ducks real good, and when you finish them off with gadwall, teal, and a few geese in the spread, you can do really good in the prairie or marsh."

Moore said something else you might want to consider when hunting the marsh is adding confidence decoys: "I always put out a great blue heron decoy. Those herons are smart birds, and ducks know that if everything is cool with them, it should be safe. Also, I sometimes throw in coots for good measure. There are lots of coots at times."

- You can make decoys look a lot more lifelike by rigging a line of them on a pull cord. When you see ducks in the distance, start pulling on the cord to create additional movement in your spread.

- Getting up early in the morning and expecting the geese to fly at dawn is not necessarily something hunters should expect to experience on public lands. Quite often, the best flight is around 10 a.m., when many hunters are already heading back home frustrated with the lack of action.

"These geese are not stupid," said waterfowl Clint Starling of Pasadena. "They have figured out the patterns of the hunters much better than we have them, and one of the things I really try to do is to stick it out and wait for the late shooting action, because more often than not, it pays off."

Chapter Eleven

Gearing up for Waterfowl

The pursuit of waterfowl requires an investment in more gear than just about any other type of hunting. When I load up for a duck or goose hunt, I am frequently astounded at the massive amount of stuff I end up bringing with me.

I have always said there are two kinds of outdoorsmen: The wildlife guys who do it mainly for the encounter with game and the overall adventure; and the gear guys whose No. 1 reason for taking up outdoors sports is all of the cool gadgets that go along with it. That does not mean that gear guys do not like wildlife and wildlife guys do not like gear. Each segment is necessary to the other.

I am undoubtedly a wildlife person, and I admit gear people probably end up being more consistent waterfowlers, if only because their attention to detail with equipment is so strong.

Gear guys read on and marvel at the myriad equipment choices available to waterfowlers. For those on the wildlife side, take notes; the forthcoming section includes many things you will need to make a successful hunt.

Guns & Loads

There have been volumes written about selecting the right shotgun and shells for wing-shooting. And, frankly, most of it has not been practical for the average hunter not interested in the highly detailed nuances of various products. What most hunters want to know is what it will take to get the job done, and where to start to gear up for waterfowling. I am the last person to want to get into a long, drawn-out dialogue over ballistic efficiency and why one brand of shotgun is better than another. I have owned five different brands and they all killed birds. With that established, this chapter should help get you started if you are new to waterfowl hunting, and provide fresh insights to those who have been at this for a long time.

Waterfowl Guns

There are three types of shotguns in common circulation today: pump, semi-automatic, and break-open (single shot and double barrel). There are bolt-action shotguns, and at least two manufacturers offered them as "goose guns" with 30-inch barrels, but few hunters use them anymore.

Of these configurations, the pump is by far the most popular, least expensive, and highly durable. That is a big plus for hunters like me who are terrible on their equipment. Pumps can survive infrequent oiling and going through the worst of what duck and goose habitat has to offer. Since pumps require the hunter to "pump" each round into the chamber, it does take a little time between shots. Some hunters dislike this while others believes it give them extra time to focus on a second shot. This is also a great function for young waterfowlers, as the hunter cannot just pull the trigger and fire again. That is what semi-automatics offer.

Side-by-sides have a loyal but small following in Texas, but in other parts of the country, they are quite popular.

If you had asked me what I thought of semi-autos 10 years ago, I would have told you they are pieces of junk that do not hold up to real field usage and jam all the time, causing me to miss some great opportunities. Modern incarnations of these fast-firing guns are much more reliable, although they do require far more attention than pump guns. Another advantage is they are generally a little easier on the shoulder, as many are gas operated and reduce recoil significantly. There are also recoil-operated guns that use the kick to work the action.

Break-open guns are not very popular with duck hunters in Texas, but they do have a following. I am not personally a big fan because the few that I have used left bruises the size of the Anahuac National Wildlife Refuge on my shoulder. I field-tested a side-by-side that performed like a dream, but

PHOTO BY ROGER BACON

It's important for a hunter to have a gun that is comfortable and designed for the kind of hunting he will do.

brutalized me. One serious advantage they do offer is safety. If the gun is broken open, it is in 100 percent safe mode.

The 12-gauge is the standard for waterfowl hunting. It provides the most versatility in terms of action, power, and ability to get the job done for a variety of applications, from giant geese to tiny teal and everything between. These guns are powerful, and no matter where you go, you can generally find a load that fits your situation. Hold that thought, because we will discuss loads in detail a bit farther on.

Some hunters prefer the smaller 20-gauge for duck hunting, particularly during the early teal season. I am not a big fan of the 20-gauge for duck hunting, and recommend them mainly for youngsters getting into the sport who will be shooting at birds only at close range.

The 10-gauge has become increasingly popular, and if you want to kill something and make sure it is dead, this is your gun. Shells are expensive, and so is the toll on your shoulder, even if the gun is adequately padded. Most of the time, these guns are for serious goose hunters, as the gun gives a little extra range and power to knock down these tough and alert birds. I know a few guys who use them for ducks, and I have seen little greenwings whacked at close range. It is not pretty.

Something to consider when selecting a shotgun is that most models are for medium to large men. There are youth and ladies models that have a shorter stock, which makes them much easier to use for those without huge arms. Consider these when introducing someone into the sport. Just because a kid says he can handle your gun does not mean it is the best option available.

CHOKE SYSTEMS

Most shotguns come with an interchangeable choke system, which controls the shot dispersal pattern. The choke "tubes" thread into the last 1 to 3 inches of the barrel. The three common types are Full, Modified, and Improved or Improved Cylinder.

The good folks at Mossberg explain that a Full (tight) constriction controls the fired pellets to a narrow column for the longer distance: "The Modified is a medium, all-purpose setting between Full and Improved Cylinder. The Improved Cylinder is a more open constriction that allows the pellets to spread sooner, and in a wider circle.

"The term 'fixed choke barrel' means the choke constriction is pre-machined into the barrel at the factory; no choke adjustments can be made. Before interchangeable choke tube systems became popular, most barrels were fixed choke types. Fixed choke barrels are still offered on guns made for specific shooting purposes; their barrels will be stamped with their specific choke constriction.

"The majority of today's shotguns feature an interchangeable choke tube system. Instead of fixing the choke in the barrel, each choke tube is internally machined to a specific choke dimension. This convenience allows the shooter to perhaps use the Full tube for waterfowl in the morning, and simply change the choke tube (instead of the gun or barrel) for different game that afternoon."

To check how your gun is patterning, Mossberg recommends hanging up a large piece of paper (approximately 40x40 inches) with an "X" marked in the middle to aim at: "Pace off the approximate distance you expect your target will be from you (35 yards is a good starting point). Use the same ammo you expect to hunt with and fire one round. On the target, write your distance, ammo brand, shot size, and other pertinent information such as wind and weather conditions, because you won't remember later. Using the same ammo, hang a new target paper, install a different choke tube, and fire another round, again writing all of your notes on the paper target.

"In addition to your pattern results, you might also notice you're shooting a little to the left, right, up, or down; adjust your sights or point of aim to compensate. Move forward or back by 10 yards and repeat your tests. Performing this type of test allows you to see, compare, and understand the performance of your gun. Perform pattern tests with different ammo and choke tubes to fine-tune your shotgun. The only way to really know what kind of a pattern you're getting from each tube and ammo is to pattern test."

NON-TOXIC SHOT

Since lead shot was banned in the 1990s, hunters have been relegated to using steel shot for the most part—and in my ever-so-humble opinion, it sucks.

Steel is somewhere around 70 percent as dense as lead, so shot of the same size is worlds apart in terms of energy delivered to the target. Shooting writer Layne Simpson wrote an article noting that if you shoot No. 4 pellets of lead and of steel from a shotgun, they both leave the barrel at around 1350 feet per second. However at around the 40-yard range, lead delivers 4.4 foot-pounds of energy, while steel gives only about 2.4 foot pounds. This means hunters would have to use No. 2 steel to deliver 4.4 foot-pounds at that range to do the same job as No. 4 lead.

Simpson wrote: "Even when larger pellets are used, ammo loaded with steel shot does not equal the performance of lead shot loads at all ranges, simply because a shotshell of a given length is incapable of holding as many of the larger steel pellets. Staying with those same two shot sizes in our comparison, Winchester offers 2-1/4 ounces of No. 4 lead shot in its 12-gauge 3-1/2-inch turkey load, for a total count of 303 pellets. That same company's 3-1/2-inch waterfowl load is capable of holding only 1-9/16 ounces of No. 2 steel, for a total of 195 pellets. Even though the steel shot load delivers the same amount of energy per pellet, its effective range is considerably less simply because a pattern fired with it contains only 65 percent as many pellets."

Does this mean you should not use steel? No, it does not. Many of us cannot afford the other nontoxic shots that are available.

If you are using steel from a .12 gauge, which is what I will be profiling, I recommend No. 4 shot for teal, bufflehead, and other small ducks, and No. 2 shot for big ducks. For geese, go with BBB or BB.

Bismuth, in my opinion, is great. It is a lot closer to the density of lead. Steel can do a lot of damage to a shotgun barrel, particularly on models manufactured before it was required. Bismuth does not cause these same problems, and delivers a serious wallop. Use No. 4 or No. 5 shot for ducks and No. 1 for geese.

Tungsten-Matrix is even closer to the density of lead than Bismuth, and is great for use in older guns. Most of the hunters I know that use this stuff rave about the pattern it holds and its overall performance. Use No. 3 shot for ducks (6 for early teal) and No. 1 for geese. Tungsten-Iron is also available and quite popular in northern markets. I have never personally used it, but I have read that No. 4 is best for ducks and No. 2 for geese. This hard material delivers a serious wallop at long distances.

Hevi-Shot is another nontoxic alternative recommended by Simpson: "Hevi-Shot as now loaded by Remington is the newest player in the nontoxic-shot game. Composed of tungsten, nickel, and iron, it is the heaviest of the nontoxics. At a density of 12.0 gms/cc, it is heavier even than lead. Owing to its extreme hardness, Hevi-Shot should be used only in guns designed to handle steel shot. Ducks of all sizes solidly hit inside 30 yards exploded like feather pillows in midair, but, more importantly, each and every shooter there made dead-in-the-air kills at ranges for which steel would have consistently crippled at best. I like No. 6 for turkeys and ducks, No. 4 for small geese, and No. 2 for Canadas."

The Hevi-Shot manufacturer notes that the shot can produce cosmetic rub marks in barrels and chokes, simply a change in surface finish: "Over an equal number of rounds, this rubbing is similar to that experienced with steel shot. Both materials create more choke strain than lead shot due to a more solid payload. With the Remington wad column, the Hevi-Shot pellets rest on a cushioned pad in the shot container that allows the pellets to flow better through the choke."

CLOTHING

Dressing for waterfowl-hunting success requires two very important elements: camouflage and climate comfort.

Ducks and geese have very sharp eyes and can pick out just about anything that doesn't belong. Hunters must go to great lengths to avoid being spotted, particularly late in the season when the birds are super wary from being have steel thrown at them at every stop.

Any camouflage pattern that breaks up your outline will get the job done. I say this first because I am not about to insult your intelligence by saying the simple military-style patterns used for years all of a sudden do not work anymore. They do. I do not believe they are the best option in many situations, but I have hunted with them myself in the past and went home with plenty of ducks.

Wetlands and marsh grass-style patterns are best for hunting in marshes and flooded prairies. They mimic closely the winter vegetation patterns for these environments and give hunters an edge. Camouflage is all about matching one's surroundings, so one pattern does not fit all. If you are goose hunting, for example, and lying in the middle of hundreds of white decoys, a long white goose-hunting trench coat with a matching headpiece and gloves might be the way to go. However, if you are hunting in the timber and standing against cypress trees or tupelo gums, then dark patterns, like

Camouflage (even on the face) is crucially important to fooling waterfowl.

those used for deer hunting, and military patterns will do just fine.

Out of all of the camouflage you might have on your body, the most important is a facemask. More missed opportunities arise when hunters look up at the birds without having their faces camouflaged. Either have a good ski mask or lightweight hood, or paint your face with a mixture of dark colors. This *is* necessary.

Wear gloves, as your hands can give you away as well. If you are hunting in either a mosquito-laden area or in cold weather, you will be glad you have on gloves. I like to wear lightweight Gore-Tex gloves, as they allow me to pull the trigger easily and load shells without any problems. A thick pair of mittens does not allow that.

The key to staying comfortable is to pay attention to the climate you will be hunting. In Texas, it is extremely important to dress in layers. Often, the weather is cold early and then warms up considerably within a couple of hours. Do not just wear a huge jumpsuit adequate for hunting the arctic. Dress in a heavy but light jacket, with a thick shirt under that, and then thermals under that. For bottoms, thermals, a light pair of pants, and neoprene waders should be enough for just about any weather in the Lone Star State. If you dress this way, you can easily remove some of the layers if you get too hot, which is likely to happen.

Precipitation is an important consideration when dressing. We have already covered that waders will keep most of you dry. A Gore-Tex jacket with a hood will do the same for the rest of your body, as will a good poncho. Always carry a poncho with you, as they are lightweight and take up very little room, and can save the day when the rain is pouring.

Finally, of the greatest inventions of all time for hunters, in my opinion, are the little packets of hand and feet warmers that make your layered clothing super effective. They come in lightweight packets you simply squeeze and shake to cause a chemical reaction that can keep you warm when nothing else will. I highly recommend buying a bulk supply before the season and keeping them with you at all times in the field. You never know when you will need them.

WADERS

Waders are an essential component of duck hunting that allow the hunter to stay dry and warm in wet, frigid environments. They are essentially overalls with boots attached. They come in three varieties: rubber, neoprene, and Gore-Tex.

Rubber waders are lightweight and work great for the early teal season and much of the general duck season, when temperatures average from the upper 30s to the 60s. They also run cheap these days. Rubber waders come in the chest variety, which fit right under your arms, and the hip style, which as the name implies fits up the legs to the hips like extra-long boots; they are sometimes called "hip boots" or "wading boots."

Waders allow hunters to stay dry and warm in the most inhospitable conditions.

Neoprene waders are more on the costly side, but are generally more comfortable and better for hunting in the cold. Neoprene waders have a much tighter fit and are far more flexible than rubber. Disadvantages include difficult to patch in the event of a puncture, and many brands do not come with shoes made into them; you therefore have to buy separate shoes or boots.

Gore-Tex waders are made from a flexible, breathable material that works great for Texas climates. Your sweat can pass through the material, but it keeps water on the outside from getting in. They are a little pricey, but worth the investment.

LANYARDS & STRAPS

Do not attempt to carry ducks or geese out of the field without a good lanyard or "duck strap" (hence the term, "strap of ducks"). You will end up spending most of your time picking up birds that fall out of your hands.

A lanyard is essentially a necklace that has spaces fixed to hold birds by the head. They are not fancy, but are important for making the end of your hunt easier and keeping you out of trouble. On group hunts, game wardens demand that ducks and geese are separated by individual hunter's limits, so lanyards can save you from getting a ticket.

There are two types of lanyards. One is what I call a "loop lanyard," which has a bunch of little loops to hang the birds by. Then there is what I call the "metal lanyard," which is made of rope or sometimes heavy-neoprene and connects to two large metal grooves in which you can slide the bird's neck. I prefer the latter for their ease of use and because they allow much more room for bigheaded geese.

There are also lanyards designed specifically for carrying calls into the field. Most of them are loop lanyards, but designed for one call. Others can hold up to a half dozen calls.

A good strap provides an easy way to sort and organize ducks in the field.

FOOD AND BEVERAGES

It is important to bring along food and beverages on a waterfowl hunt, as you will expend a lot of energy that needs to be replaced.

Ideally, you will be in a cozy blind where someone can cook up sausage and eggs. I have experienced this kind of spoiled hunting on a couple of occasions, and must say that I quite enjoyed it. Most times, however, you will need to pack lightweight, high-energy food that will keep you warm and alert. I recommend protein bars, which are available at most grocery stores now. They are a great choice because they tend to have a good mix of protein and carbohydrates and they will fill you up quickly. They are easy to pack and take up very little space. Sandwiches are an easy to carry choice as well, and require no special trip to the grocery store.

In my opinion, what you carry in the field to eat is not quite as important as what you eat before you get there. Do not eat super high fiber goods before you go to bed or for breakfast. They will send you running to the bathroom, and in most waterfowl hunting situations, that is extremely inconvenient.

I am not a coffee drinker, but for those who do like a cup of java, a thermos with your favorite blend can go a long way toward making a cold hunt a pleasant one. I prefer hot chocolate and always stock up on it before the hunting season begins. It is my waterfowl hunting addiction.

I also like to carry Gatorade or other power drinks because they replace the electrolytes we lose in the field. In fact, I usually end every hunt with one of these and find that it gives me the energy to face the rest of the day, and—more importantly—get up to make another hunt.

Do not let the process of selecting gear overwhelm you. You will hear and read a lot of debates over guns, loads, and everything else in the world of waterfowl. In reality, you can follow the simple guidelines used here to have success in the field repeatedly.

Chapter Twelve

Blinds of All Shapes & Sizes

Duck and goose blinds come in just about every shape and form the imagination can conjure. I have been in blinds that had heaters and stoves, and in a tiny one that I had to pull a banded water snake out of before I got in. There are big blinds, little blinds, gaudy blinds, and bizarre blinds.

The best place to start is where many waterfowlers began hunting: natural cover.

NATURAL BLINDS

Along the Texas coast, stands of roseau cane make excellent natural blinds. It grows along the shorelines of bays and in the marshes, and very often is thick along the points that make the best hunting. Many times, I have simply pulled back the cane, stepped inside, and started hunting. This cane is very useful in camouflaging a boat as well. I always bring along a cane knife or machete, and if necessary, pull my boat as close to shore as I can and surround it with cane. The advantage of this is that it is free and you can exactly match your immediate surroundings.

Around farm ponds and in freshwater systems, cattail stands make great natural blinds. They are usually thick enough to hide a well-camouflaged hunter, and are actually quite comfortable. I actually fell asleep in some cattails during one early teal season, and awakened to find a pond full of teal in front of me.

In the timber and along the reservoirs, simple brush and dead trees can make great cover. Anything that will cover the outline and movement of the hunter will get the job done. As I write this chapter, I think of a great natural brush blind on a friend's deer lease in Newton County provided by Hurricane Rita. It is a big pine along a slough that fell across a medium-sized oak. The way it is set up, it covers our tops but it allows us to shoot above, and gives us a perfect shooting window toward the slough.

Using natural cover is the most common way to hunt on refuge land.

Abandoned manmade structures can make good blinds if they are in good locations. While pike fishing on Skaneatles Lake in New York, I saw an old boat wreck duck hunters were using. It had been drug into the shallows and was covered with brush. Apparently, it was set up right along a flyway and the hunters simply sat in it and shot ducks and geese as they flew over.

On farms, there always seems to be an abandoned tractor or truck, and if placed in the right location, they make good blinds. The birds are used to seeing this kind of thing, and do not seem to mind their presence.

PORTABLE BLINDS

Over the last few years, I have used portable ground blinds like the Double Bull to hunt ducks.

By using portable ground blinds, which you can set up in less than five minutes, you can play the wind and sun to set up exactly where you need to be.

Portable blinds like this one are usually used for deer hunting but they can double for duck blinds if needed.

Most of the time, these blinds are used by bowhunters, and in fact, that is why I bought one, but they are great for waterfowl, too.

Veteran bowhunter Mike Cascio gave me a great tip for using ground blinds. Since most of them have black lining, he advised wearing black shirts, gloves, and facemask or makeup. "That pretty much renders you as invisible," he said.

There are dozens of portable ground blinds on the market. You will have to figure out which one best suit your needs but most of them are affordable and can be adapted for waterfowling needs.

Boat Blinds

Probably the most common blind choice for hunters is their boats. If you are hunting on the main body of a reservoir or in a bay, it is not always possible to have an actual blind. Boats come in handy in these situations. Some hunters, as mentioned earlier, simply cover their boats with cane, while others use material called "fast grass." It is literally woven marsh grass (or a synthetic) that goes around the boat to make it look like a natural structure. There are other options, like the Flexi-Blind that has spring loaded support poles that bring up camouflage netting or canvas to hide the boat. These units can be pricey, but are generally convenient.

Pit Blinds

My favorite type of blind, which is commonly used in agricultural fields and marshes, is the pit blind. They are usually made of concrete or a hard plastic and sunk into the ground in a key waterfowl feeding area or travel route. These blinds require serious labor to install and are generally used on private leases where there will be a lot of hunting. Otherwise, they are not worth the effort.

PHOTO COURTESY OF THE U.S. FISH AND WILDLIFE SERVICE

Pit blinds allow hunters to actually go into the earth to ambush ducks and geese. They are comfortable and offer great concealment.

The advantages of pit blinds are that they provide good cover by allowing you to get under the ground to an extent, and give you good footing in a normally squishy area. Disadvantages are that they collect rainwater and sometimes the creatures of the wetlands. I once heard a story of a Louisiana hunter who had a big nutria climb in the pit with him before daylight. As the story goes, the hunter sees the form of something in the pre-dawn light, and when he turned on the flashlight, all he could see was fur and those nasty orange teeth. He got so freaked out he decided to go home.

All I have to say is that hunter must not have been a true Cajun, else that nutria would have become something to cook with the duck.

PLATFORM BLINDS

Platform blinds require a lot of work to put up but they are sturdy and comfortable.

Platform blinds are common in many areas. They are usually a simple wooden frame that emerges from the water and is covered with natural brush. These are common on reservoirs and along the coast. In fact, from Port O'Connor southward, you can hardly find an area on the bay where they are not a part of the scenery.

LAYOUT BLINDS

Layout blinds are common in dry ground hunting for geese. The Avery Migrator is a prime example. When folded, it fits easily into a short wheel base pickup truck; the folded measurements are 65 inches long, 38 inches wide, and 5 inches tall. Features include a 22-pound weight, angled zippered flagging ports, padded seat and headrest, padded barrel rest, zippered boot bag for easy clean-up, rear ventilation window, offset doors to eliminate shadows, and camouflage straps.

These types of blinds are awesome for hunting inside a goose spread, as they cover you entirely and allow you to pop up at the last second for a shot. My first experience with them was on a dry ground hunt for Canadas, and I could not believe how close the birds approached. It was awesome!

Another cool portable that Avery puts out is the Neotub, which allows hunters to sort of lie down and stay dry in the water. The NeoTub's bottom is made from waterproof 3mm neoprene with an almost indestructible 600D polyester laminated outer layer. The sides and top are constructed from the same 3mm camo neoprene that your favorite waders are made of. All

Blinds that allow hunters to lie down and pop up when the birds show up are becoming increasingly popular.

seams are glued and blind stitched just like waders. It is perfect for hunting surface water, flooded cornfields, rice fields, and soybean fields.

DIY Temporary Blinds

For hunters interested in building their own temporary blind, Ducks Unlimited has provided an easy step-by-step system.

Materials:
- *6 wooden fence posts*
- *12 yards of woven fencing wire*
- *one 4x8-foot sheet of 1/2-inch plywood*
- *1 pound of framing nails*
- *one package of black cable ties.*

Required tools included a sledgehammer, standard hammer, ax, chain saw, and wire cutters.

Step 1: *First, we positioned the blind where we had seen most of the mallards working. Prevailing winds in this area blow from the southwest and northwest, so we faced the blind to the northeast. Ducks gliding in on the former wind would offer a head-on shot; on the latter wind, a right-to-left crossing shot. Also, facing northeast, we did not have to worry about looking into the sun. We began construction by driving three fence posts into the mud (ends sharpened with the ax) in a straight line with a spacing of 4 feet between each post. Then we drove the other three posts in a parallel line 4 feet behind the first line. The result was a six-post rectangle, 8 feet long by 4 feet wide.*

Step 2: *Next, we cut off the posts 4 feet high with the chainsaw. Then we encased the frame with the hog wire, stretching and nailing the wire onto the posts as we unrolled it. We left one end un-nailed for entry/exit. Adding the wire* *provided form and strength to our blind, tying all the posts together.*

Step 3: *Next, we cut small bushy oak trees around the edge of the field and stood them up around the blind to totally conceal the posts and wire. We secured the little trees to the wire with cable ties. We also arranged the trees in front and back, so limbs intermeshed over the top of the blind, providing overhead cover for the shooting stations.*

Step 4: *Finally, we sawed the plywood sheet in half to use as a makeshift floor. We simply laid the plywood atop the mud, and our weight pushed it a couple of inches into the gumbo. This provided a solid base for our folding stools and for standing to shoot. We still had water up to our ankles, but our insulated rubber boots warded off any discomfort or inconvenience.*

Our final touch was driving a couple of nails into each post to serve as hangers for shell bags, binoculars, and other accessories we needed to keep out of the water.

With this setup, we were able to hunt exactly where the ducks wanted to work. By wearing full camo and keeping still in the shadows of the oak branches, we were hidden from their overhead searching eyes. For two weeks, until the water finally came up to float our big blind, we enjoyed some wonderful shooting in this setup. After a couple of swings, most ducks were convinced all was safe, and they fell right into the spread.

No matter what kind of blind you use, make sure and set it up in the right location. Remember the wind should come from behind the blind because ducks like to fly into the wind, and it will give you a good chance at making fatal frontal shots as well as make it easier to identifying the ducks.

Sun is also important to consider. If the sun will be directly in your face and the ducks fly in that area just as the sun starts really illuminating the surroundings, you might want to make adjustments.

Finally, if you already have a duck blind, there are things you can do to make it better. According to DU:

Building a better duck blind is all about having the right perspective—that of a duck in flight rather than your own earthbound view. Think back over last season. If circling ducks frequently appeared to shy away from your blind, you might want to make some changes.

If, for instance, birds often landed wide of your blind, maybe you should rethink your brushing strategy, modify the width of the shooting box, lower the overall height of the blind, or possibly even relocate it. (Sometimes, ducks land around the next bend in the creek simply because that particular spot—even though only 80 yards from your decoys—naturally appeals to them.) Now is the time to decide what, if any, changes should be made, and to get on with the work.

Blinds are just another part of the puzzle that is necessary for doing duck business. Whether you hunt out of your boat, on the land, or in a huge pit blind, you are using a tool that enhances the odds of having fried duck breast in the pan. And they are just like anything else, the more work you put into them, the better off you will be when the decisive moment arrives.

Chapter Thirteen

Duck Hunting Boats

Boats and waterfowl hunting go hand in hand. The fact that most opportunities are in aquatic environments makes a boat an almost essential tool in the hunter's kit. Fortunately for hunters, there are many options available, ranging from the simple and inexpensive all the way up to the complex and break-the-bank level.

Let's take a look at the most popular boats available to Texas waterfowlers, so you can figure out which is best for you.

A good dog will have no problem maneuvering from boat to water.

Pirogues

Smokey Crabtree has hunted, fished, and trapped the Sulphur River bottoms his entire life. Now 79 years young, the Fouke, Arkansas, native and author of *Smokey and the Fouke Monster* and *The Man Behind the Legend* told me much of his hunting was done in a simple pirogue.

"A lot of guys like to go a couple of hundred yards into the woods and set up," Crabtree said. "That's fine, but if they would get them a pirogue and paddle into the swamps, they would do much better."

Pirogues have been a valuable tool for hunting for hundreds of years throughout the South. The original pirogue was a tiny boat carved from a cypress log. The Cajun people of Louisiana popularized it.

"Pirogues are super-versatile and quiet boats that allow hunters to slip into areas without making a lot noise, and get into areas a lot of other boats can't," said Morgan Perrin if the Lodge of Louisiana.

Piroughes are usually wooden but there are plastic versions like this one. They were first designed by Cajuns navigating shallow bayous.

Perrin's ancestors helped to settle the town of Lafitte, and according to him, there is no telling how many ducks and alligators hunters have bagged from the tiny boats: "It would probably blow your mind if you knew how much game has been transported on pirogues. And they're still in use today."

Indeed they are.

"Big" Mac Owen, one of the original Duck Men from the popular video series, helped refine the modern pirogue.

Duck Commander produces the result of refinements—aluminum pirogues lighter than wood, stronger than fiberglass, and that will not rot. One of their more popular models, the Black Water Pirogue, has a 500-pound capacity and can navigate as little as 2 inches of water.

JOHNBOATS/MUDBOATS

I do most of my boat-in hunting from a 16-foot flat-bottomed Grumman johnboat. Propelled by a 25-horsepower Mercury outboard with shallow-water drive capabilities, I can navigate shallow water even with a heavy load. Johnboats are great for duck hunting, and are roomy enough to make great duck blinds.

My cousin, Frank Moore, and I cut bamboo poles out of a woodlot near my home, affix them to my boat as a frame, drape military netting around it, park against a bank with high cane, and blend right in. We shoot many ducks this way, and do not have to go through the trouble of setting up blinds. By using the boat, we are mobile and can move to where the birds are with little trouble. You can read much more about this in the Blinds chapter.

Standard johnboats are great for hunting open, deep water on bays and on the main body of large reservoirs. Johnboats can also become "mudboats" to navigate shallow marshes if they are equipped with specialized outboards.

Webster's dictionary defines a mudboat as "a large flatboat used in

Boats quite often double as blinds for hunters.

dredging." A growing number of sportsmen along the coast define mudboats as essential tools for getting into remote hunting and fishing locations they never dreamed they could reach. The boat itself is not that important. Just about any flat-bottom aluminum rig will get the job done if it has a true "mud motor" to push it. Specialized motors and skinny-water vessels make the combination we call the "mudboat" a reality.

First up is the Go-Devil. Manufactured by Warren Coco of Baton Rouge, Louisiana, the Go-Devil is unique in that the prop is mounted on a long rod that allows the pilot to instantly adjust for depth. This permits navigation in areas with virtually no water——a necessary endeavor in many waterfowl hunting situations.

Outdoors lovers have used the Go-Devil since 1977. Go-Devil Inc. distributes to every state and province in North America. Many duck hunters call them the "four-wheel drive" of marine engines, and for good reason. These contraptions go over mud, rocks, stumps, and just about anything else. According to the manufacturer, a Go-Devil needs about 9 inches of soft bottom to start from a standstill. That can be 1 inch of water and 8 eight inches of mud. Once the boat is running on plane, it can run in about 1/4-inch of water in soft mud or 9 inches over a hard bottom.

Go-Devils clamp on the transom like a regular tiller-steered outboard motor, so there is no need to drill boltholes in your transom. Go-Devils can run on boats with 15- to 17-inch high transoms. The ideal transom height is 16 inches.

"I love these motors because they allow me to go into areas a lot of other hunters can't reach," said Robert Brown of Orange. "I hunt public land a lot, and there are some ponds on the areas I hunt that I couldn't get to if I didn't have one of these motors. This puts me away from the crowds and into some prime duck hunting."

I have hunted with Brown and his Go-Devil-equipped boat on several occasions. I was impressed with the ease of navigation. The marshes in the Lower Neches Wildlife Management Area where we hunt are some of the most difficult to navigate in the state, if not the country. The mud is soft and deep, and the water is super-shallow. Some of the best hunting areas are within walking distance, but there is no way a man can make the trek without becoming a permanent part of the marsh.

I grew up hunting and fishing in those marshes, and just accepted the fact if you stepped in the wrong spot, you would be in mud up to your shoulders. While hunting with Middle Coast Waterfowlers a few years ago, I got this strange look when I mentioned that I hunted that marsh. One of them told me that was by far the thickest, nastiest mud he had ever experienced, and would never hunt there again.

For years, there was one particular pond I had wanted to hunt but could never get to with my 25-horsepower Mercury outboard, and I was not nearly stupid enough to try walking out there. Brown's Go-Devil took us there with no problem, and allowed us to shoot ducks in an area where few others had success.

"My Go-Devil has really made hunting a lot easier and got me into areas I never thought I could get into before," Brown said.

Go-Devils will run a regular flat-bottomed boat, but the manufacturer says you will get better performance with a Go-Devil Boat. The company designs them for use with Go-Devil engines. They come armed with a slick bottom and round chine that allow them to slide through mud and over logs and stumps.

James Warlock of Houston said his Go-Devil helps him reach some

Go-devils are the most popular shallow water driving motors for duck hunters.

of the desolate areas in the San Jacinto and Trinity River bottoms: "Coastal marsh is one thing. It is usually just smooth mud and grass, but the bottoms are an entirely different issue with lots of logs and snags. I am able to go right over a lot of these obstructions without much problem. That's crucial where I hunt."

Warlock said his boat allows him to reach an area on his hunting club that no other hunters fool with: "They always ask me how I bag the big bucks and come home with lots of mallards and wood ducks. I tell them it's because

I hunt by boat and go where they don't go."

Next up is the Pro-Drive outboard. A few years ago, I had the pleasure of trying one out during the first-ever Texas field test of the product. The Pro-Drive is equipped with an electric clutch for instant forward or neutral, providing maximum maneuverability, handling, and safety. As I saw in the marsh, there is no need to lean out over the side of the boat when turning. The engine's tight turning radius assists when navigating through trails and tight spaces. We traveled across slippery mud flats without losing speed, having to stand, or adjusting the motor.

The gear reduction ratio of 1.5:1 allows the Pro-Drive to turn a large propeller, giving superior performance in the mud. An adjustable trim provides additional control and eliminates tiller handle torque, making longer trips much less tiring. The trim also allows you to keep the propeller running at the surface of the water or mud, reducing strain on the engine and wear on the propeller.

A 25-horsepower Kohler engine powers the Pro-Drive, which weighs about 200 pounds. The lower unit gearbox is well above the bottom of the boat, leaving only the skeg plate and half of the prop below the boat bottom. The only area affected when hitting stumps or logs is the bottom skeg. The motor kicks up freely when crossing over logs and other obstructions. As a demonstration, we stopped in the middle of a flat with absolutely no water on it and shut down the motor. We then started it back up, wiggled a little, and got up and going with no problem.

The unit retails for a little over $4000 and is available through Beta Marine in Groves. According to manager Jude Peek: "We're really excited about offering this product. The speed and handling are something I don't think many hunters and fishermen would expect from a product like this, but it is here, and most of the people who have tried it out have found it quite amazing."

Pro-drives are fairly new on the market and can run across almost any kind of wet surface.

AIRBOATS

Airboats allow even greater access to distant hunting areas, and are a blast to ride. They can travel across deep water or literally dry land. Stan Floyd, owner of American Airboats, said the airboat is the ultimate in hunting rides: "If you want to get out to the remote areas, the airboat is the way to do it."

I fell in love with airboats when Floyd took me frogging nearly a decade ago. We used the machine to navigate a huge, shallow lake and grabbed frogs by hand.

"Compared to powerboats and wheeled vehicles, airboats are environmentally friendly," Floyd said. "With no props in the water to damage fish, manatees, and underwater vegetation, and no wheels or tracks to dig into the wetlands, airboats leave no scar on the landscape. An hour after the airboat has left an area, there is very little trace that it had ever been there. There are no ruts or other scars on the land, and no oily residues in the water. Most airboats are powered by clean-burning four-cycle engines. With above-the-water exhaust, no pollutants such as oil, exhaust fumes, or unburned fuel are deposited in the water."

Floyd said stripped down racing airboats can reach speeds over 135 miles per hour on smooth, shallow water, and can reach this speed in 4 seconds (1/8-mile).

According to an article in U.S. Airboat magazine: "Speeds over 60 mph in any watercraft can be risky and is not recommended. The same is true for automobiles. The differences are: roads are much more uniform than waterways, and unlike cars, most watercraft do not have brakes."

Air boats are noisy and cumbersome but they allow anglers to get into areas most other boats can't reach.

Floyd holds the official land speed record of 47.76 mph, which was set at the Houston International Dragway in September 1995.

"Forty-eight milers per hour and an elapsed quarter mile time of 21.26 seconds doesn't sound that fast, until you consider that it was set in a standard 300 horsepower, three-seat airboat not a stripped down hot-rod," Floyd said. "The record was also set on asphalt. Going across a grassy meadow, this airboat could easily top 55 miles per hour."

Popular with duck hunting guides on the middle Texas Coast, airboats are not only the ultimate shallow-water craft, they are fast and roomy as well. The only real drawback is that airboats are deafeningly loud and passengers must wear hearing protection.

Airboats are used not only on the coast, but also as far north in Texas as the Brazos River, where some duck hunters use them to run semi-dry creek beds.

HOVERCRAFT

The next step in shallow water navigation is the hovercraft, which literally hovers above the water's surface. There are not many of them on the market specifically geared for hunting, but Hovercraft of Arkansas offers a Sportsman's series that comes decked out in camouflage ready for hunting.

Hovercraft fly a few inches off the surface on a cushion of air. They will fly over any relatively smooth surface, including water, grass, ice, and snow. Speed depends on surface conditions. Ice is an efficient surface and speeds reach 60 mph or more. Long grass is porous and a lot of lift is lost, so the hover height is lower. Skirt drag is greater so speed is reduced to as little as 20 mph. Hovercraft are relatively quiet and make a worthy conveyance for hunters who dislike the noise of airboats.

I am a hunter that likes to get into the most remote areas I can possibly find. This might have as much to do with my desire to tread where few have dared, but it is also practical from a hunting standpoint. I experience the best hunting in these quiet areas, surrounded by water and shielded from civilization. Without boats, we would have to be content to simply wonder what dwells in these areas.

That is not an option I can live with.

Hovercrafts have not really caught on in Texas but they do have a cult following for their ability to negotiate pretty much any kind of surface.

HUNTING BOAT MANUFACTURERS

Duck Commander Pirogues, 877-396-7612,
www.duckcommander.com

Landau Boats, 417-532-9126, www.landauboats.com

Go-Devil, 888-490-3254, www.go-devil.com

American Airboats, 800-241-6390, www.americanairboats.com

Hovercraft of Arkansas, 501-982-3579,
www.usamarineservice.com

Amphibious Marine (hovercraft), 360-426-3170,
www.amphibiousmarine.com

Chapter Fourteen

Geese, geese, & more geese

At first, I thought I was seeing things. Just as the sun started to peek over the marsh, a large black shape blacked out the available light. Was this a fog coming from the nearby Gulf? Or a building storm?

From a distance, it looked like one giant shape, but as it approached closer, the familiar cackling sound of snow geese broke the silence of the morning. What seemed to be one huge object were actually thousands of geese moving in unison, heading in the direction of our blind. This was my first-ever real goose hunt, and the bunch I was hunting with had warned me to bring plenty of ammunition.

I am glad I did, because a combination of my poor shooting that day and many shot opportunities caused me to burn three boxes of ammo. To say we had fun is an extreme understatement.

That was many years ago, but the geese are still thick in Cameron Parish, Louisiana, where I was hunting, and throughout wintering grounds in Texas from the Panhandle to the Gulf Coast.

Snow geese sometimes roost by the hundreds of thousands. The author drove along the Sacramento National Wildlife Refuge in California in 2006 and for five miles saw nothing but white in the air.

Goose hunting is probably the most challenging aspect of the waterfowling experience, as these birds—particular snows—have super-sharp vision and wariness unmatched by most game birds. In Texas, there are four species of geese: snow, Ross', white-fronted (specklebelly), and Canada.

For the most part, hunting is broken down into snow and Canada. No one just goes out to target Ross' and specklebelly. Ross' are tiny and always mixed with snow and specklebelly, and have a bag limit of one or two birds.

Let's start with snows first, and by saying that consistently fooling them is difficult. In fact, it seems to be getting a little harder every year along the Texas coast as the average age of the geese increases, creating a more hunter-wary population savvy to all of the tricks we employ.

The 1990s saw a waterfowl-hunting renaissance in the region, with more outfitters operating than ever due to a greatly increased number of hunters. Take Missouri for example, of which a good portion falls into the Central Flyway region. During the 1990s, the light goose harvest averaged around 11,000 birds. By the 2003-2004 season, that harvest jumped to 201,300. That's a nearly 2000 percent increase in just that one state to the north of us, and 200,000 geese that did not make it to the Lone Star State.

There have been major increases in harvest and hunter participation in virtually every state in the Flyway, which is making things hard on hunters in the southern portion, who get a shot at few geese. On top of that, the ones that do make it here get an education in survival while en route. Even in Texas, competition among hunters and pressure on the waterfowl that do make it here has increased dramatically. The number of Texas waterfowl hunters has doubled since 1990.

"There is definitely more pressure on the resources here than there has been in a long, long time," said Texas Parks & Wildlife Department (TPWD) waterfowl program leader Dave Morrison.

This is especially evident during a year when forage in the arctic nesting grounds is low and few juveniles survive to migrate south. That is exactly what happened in the 2005-2006 season. According to officials with Delta Waterfowl, much of the species' arctic nesting grounds had a heavy blanket of snow into early June. In fact, the spring nesting period that season was the coldest on record, with a good portion of the geese never getting a chance to nest.

"When you have a situation like that, it creates very challenging hunting for Texans," Morrison said. "We end up getting the mature geese that have seen it all migrating southward. Juvenile geese decoy much better than mature ones. Then you add the fact that many of the juveniles we do have get shot at before they reach us, and you can see how a difficult situation can arise."

Hunters also have to factor in that snow goose populations as a whole have dropped quite a bit over the last seven years. According to U.S. Fish and Wildlife Service (USFWS) officials, the 1998 conservation order to expand light goose hunting into the spring and allow limitless bags and the use of electronic calls is bringing the population down.

"According to mid-winter surveys, the population peaked in 1998 at more than 3 million birds. The population today is nearly 2.4 million birds. The biologists' target population is little more than a million birds," according to a USFWS report.

Yes, snow goose hunters have a lot stacked against them, but there are ways to make this difficult chore doable and even productive. As previously stated, a mature population of geese presents unique challenges to hunters. I learned this lesson while hunting with Will Beaty of Central Flyway Outfitters in Winnie, Texas.

We got out to a field at 4 a.m. to set up a huge decoy spread con-

PHOTO COURTESY OF THE U.S. FISH AND WILDLIFE SERVICE

Snow geese are probably the most difficult to hunt of waterfowl once they mature. If they numbered as low as canvasbacks for example, they would be almost impossible to kill, save for young ones.

sisting of close to 1000 shells, rags, and silhouettes. Nearby was a roost of 10,000-plus geese that had been flying right over this field. After we set up the huge spread, Beaty put us about 125 yards away from the spread itself. I questioned the logic in this, but he was confident in the tactic.

"I'm telling you, the geese will see the spread and then immediately veer away from it," Beaty told me. "Hopefully, they will veer toward us hidden in this brush, and we'll get a chance at them."

As the huge flock rose off the roost, the formerly quiet morning was filled with the near deafening sound of calling geese. About 1000 of them moved in our direction, and almost as if they had been programmed to do so, veered directly away from the decoys and flew right toward us.

"See, these birds are smart. You just have to try to be smarter than they are," Beaty said.

In general, large spreads in the fields work better than small ones do, and hunters who set up realistic spreads that show geese doing a variety of things (feeding, preening, etc.) will do much better than those with just a bunch of rags out in a field. The old adage in these parts used to be that you could put a white bucket in the field and shoot snows. That is simply not true anymore, as the species has developed a level of awareness that is second to none in the waterfowl world.

You have to know the behavior of the birds in your area. If you are hunting marsh refuges, think light and mobile. If you have access to private fields, go big and super realistic.

Mix it up with life-size, photo-realistic decoys, shells, rags, and kites. During the last few years, I have seen kites popping up more on more and goose hunts, and I believe they are one of the major keys to success, depending on wind, of course. Last year, I got to participate in a hunt for Ducks Unlimited television where our quarry was snow geese. We had lots of competition, as there were numerous highly skilled outfitters operating in the area. Our spread consisted of several strategically placed kites lined up within good shooting range of the hunters. Nearly every goose we shot went right for the kites.

I believe the geese here are driven as much by pressure as they are food availability. There are lots of outfitters and refuges along the coast. With much of individual refuges closed to hunting, they have lots of sanctuary. Nonetheless, geese can be easily decoyed if you can set up near their flyway and focus on stragglers from the group. Flocks of a dozen or two are as good as dead if you have a well-placed decoy spread and do minimal calling.

If you are hunting right along the edge of a refuge, I recommend using a couple of dozen life-sized decoys, and then have a few magnums in there to grab their attention.

"I always like to have a dozen-and-a-half snows and then throw in a

A good goose spread is varied and realistic. Sharp-eyed snows will fall for nothing less on many occasions.

few specklebellies," said veteran waterfowler Chris Phelps of Lake Charles, Louisiana, who hunts around refuge property every season. "I put the snows in a cluster, mix a couple of specks in with them, and then put the rest of my specks in a group out to the side. I have always seen the small clusters of geese like this, where you will have the specks feeding around them down here, so I try to set it up as natural as I can."

Phelps said to call light for snows, but if you see specklebellies coming in alone, turn up the volume: "You almost can't over-call the specks down here, especially if you have a young bird coming in alone. If you just give it that steady action, be ready to shoot, because I have found them very easy to bring in."

Capt. Ryan Warhola hunts around the refuges in Texas. He has had good success in bagging low flying geese on foggy days, and emphasized that hunters need to be very mindful of weather conditions: "You have to really pay attention to the weather and be prepared to leave at the last minute, because this is a matter of keying in on confused geese, and that's something you don't get a chance to do everyday."

Warhola recommended hunters get familiar with the flight patterns of the birds in the section of the refuge they want to hunt: "These birds have patterns they use quite a bit in different areas. They will do the same thing on foggy mornings, but they are not sure of their surroundings, so they are a lot easier to get. Find some good cover, like around a levee or just behind a small ridge, and use that as your signpost for shooting and calling. Once the birds get to your spot, let them have it. If the fog is high enough you can see a fair way up, you will want to take farther shots, but if it is really thick, you can make super high percentage shots at near point-blank range."

Hunting Canadas is quite similar to the pursuit of snows. In fact, many Canadas are taken every year in snow goose spreads. However, most of the directed Canada hunting is done in the Panhandle and Rolling Plains regions and there are some slight differences.

Let's take the Panhandle first. The big draw for this region is the fact that Canadas are so common, with the region holding as many as half a million of the big, beautiful birds. The species is infrequently seen in the rest of the state, and the Panhandle bag limit is always higher than the two dark geese allowed for the rest of Texas.

Most geese hang out around the irrigated cropland near towns like

Canadas are present throughout Texas but are most common in the Panhandle.

Hereford and Dalhart. They are also sometimes killed around the only natural lakes in the region, playa lakes.

According to TPWD: "Playas are shallow, circular-shaped wetlands that are primarily filled by rainfall, although some playas found in cropland settings may also receive water from irrigation runoff. Playas average slightly more than 15 acres in size."

These small lakes are loaded with ducks, and if located near a good, agricultural food source, they can be good for geese as well.

When heavily pressured on the coast, snow geese sometimes head toward the Panhandle, where there are far fewer hunters and wide open spaces. This is especially true during mild winters, so keep that in mind if the geese in your neighborhood start to disappear; they go to hang out with Canadas up north.

In country this flat and open, hunters do not always have to set up large spreads, especially if they are able to hunt in areas that no one else is hunting, which is highly possible.

Medium-sized formations of predominantly dark goose decoys mixed with some snows are great. Last season, hunters were adding mechanized decoys to the mix. It was initially for shooting mallards, which were landing and feeding with geese in dry fields, but it paid off for geese as well. The setup I hear the most about is a basic dry ground spread with hunters set up in pop-up blinds in the middle, with three mechanized mallard decoys, two set to the sides of the hunters and one just ahead of them.

"The hunting in that part of the country is just phenomenal for geese and ducks. It's really a waterfowler's paradise," said guide Roger Bacon, who drives up from East Texas every season. "One thing hunters want to do is to bring plenty of ammunition with them. Once you get west of Abilene, hardly any stores carry steel shot. Make sure and bring your own because you will probably be making a lot of shots up there."

The Rolling Plains is another great area to bag Canadas. TPWD

Don't let this pretty face fool you. Canadas are sharp birds and can become difficult to hunt when pressured.

officials estimate approximately one-third of the Rolling Plains region is used for "for intensive agriculture with a variety of different crops such as wheat, cotton, and milo. Large acreages of wheat are grown annually for harvest and winter/spring livestock grazing. The remaining two-thirds of the region is rangeland devoted to cattle ranching."

Top spots are the few flooded fields here, conservation lakes, and dry crops like peanuts. Look for the light goose hunting to be better as the season draws to an end, and the early part of the season to produce more Canadas.

Most hunters in the region prefer large spreads and might go with as few as two dozen decoys, mainly of life-sized models. Late in the season, hunters prefer smaller spreads here. Calling is not optional here, as spotting geese at a long distance and luring them in with effective goose talk is typically the way hunting goes down.

Top counties are Clay, Wichita, Archer, Throckmorton, Shackelford, Callahan, Taylor, Nolan, Coke, Sterling, Tom Green, Irion, Concho, and Runnels.

A dominant theme throughout this chapter has been the wariness of geese. That cannot be overemphasized. Hunters who want to score on any kind of goose should be well camouflaged and concealed around some kind of natural cover, or in a photo-realistic blind. More goose hunters miss shots because of not wearing a facemask or having one where there is still too much face showing. If you have any face showing, put on some dark-colored make-up and conceal yourself.

If you are hunting in dry fields, laydown blinds where you are totally concealed until the decisive moment are highly recommended. (See the Blinds chapter for details.) If you are hunting in rice fields, avoid using pit blinds that have been out all season and have had hundreds of birds shot from them. At this point, the geese know what happens there and will avoid the location at all costs. Setting up along natural cover like a levee or lying in the middle of a spread (and yes, being wet and miserable) will yield far more birds. It is also important to keep your dog at bay, as the movement of a spastic retriever can easily spoil a good late-season goose hunt.

This might all seem a bit troublesome for shooting a few birds, but those who have experienced the thrill of having dozens of geese land around you and seeing hundreds, sometimes thousands fly over in shooting range because you went the extra mile, know the rewards. Goose hunting is a lot of work, but to those of us who venture afield this time of year, it is well worth the effort.

SANDHILL CRANES

Sandhill cranes are not really waterfowl, but they fall under the same umbrella due to their grain-eating nature and propensity to hang out in the same places as geese.

Numerous high-flying flocks of sandhill cranes (*Grus canadensis*) migrate through North-Central Texas each fall and spring, often stopping to roost on wheat fields or feed on waste grains in agricultural croplands.

According to TPWD: "Winter concentrations might occur in the northwestern and western counties of North-Central Texas and provide good hunting opportunity for sportsmen. Sandhill cranes roost on shallow lakes, wet areas, or sandy streambeds, and feed in croplands during the

PHOTO COURTESY OF THE U.S. FISH AND WILDLIFE SERVICE

The sirloin of the sky! Sandhill cranes are huge birds that have about five pounds of solid breast meat that is very tasty. These birds are hard to kill and sometimes downright mean.

day on green wheat, waste grains, peanuts, berries, invertebrates, small animals, and insects. Large concentrations are also found on the High Plains, Coastal Plains, and South Texas Brush Country during the winter months."

TPWD divides the state into three sandhill crane harvest regions: Zones A, B, and C. Zone A encompasses the Panhandle and Trans Pecos. Zone B is essentially the Rolling Plains and parts of the Post Oak Savannah. Zone C is South Texas. All of the state west of Interstate 35 and Highway 290 is closed due to that being the migration route of the similar-looking and highly endangered whooping crane. There is also a closed zone around the Aransas National Wildlife Refuge.

According to TPWD this encompasses: "Everything to the Gulf of Mexico from a line beginning at the Kleberg-Nueces County line and the Gulf of Mexico, west along the county line to Park Road 22, to State Hwy. 358, to State Hwy. 286, north to IH 37, east to U.S. Hwy. 181, north and west to U.S. Hwy. 77 at Sinton, north and east along U.S. Hwy. 77 to U.S. Hwy. 87 at Victoria, east and south along U.S. Hwy. 87 to State Hwy. 35 north and east along State Hwy. 35 to the south end of Lavaca Bay Causeway, south and east along the shore of Lavaca Bay to the Port Lavaca Ship Channel, south and east along the Ship Channel to the Gulf of Mexico."

To hunt sandhills you must also get a free sandhill crane hunting permit from a TPWD license vendor. Once you get past the red tape, hunting the birds is a real hoot. They can be decoyed by putting out small groups of life-sized decoys and silhouettes, and sometimes by mixing them with a few dark goose decoys. Sandhills will respond to calls, particularly when they are lost in the fog.

Most are killed by locating flyways and pass-shooting the sharp-eyed and super tasty birds. Sandhills have about 5 pounds of solid meat on their breast, earning them the nickname "ribeye of the sky." The flavor is wonderful.

Sandhills are super tough birds and require the use of at least BB shot, although T shot seems to be the most popular load in Texas. If your gun shoots 3-1/2-inch magnums, use them, and if you have a 10-gauge break it out for sandhill season. Try to shoot the birds in the neck as not

The beak of a sandhill is a deadly weapon. Do not use dogs to retrieve them as they could easily lose an eye.

to damage any of the precious breast meat.

Also, do not bring your dog out to retrieve a wounded sandhill. These birds have sharp, powerful beaks, and they have been known to take the eyes out of a dog. You should also use caution and shoot the bird in the head when approaching instead of trying to grab them and wring their necks.

Sandhills might come from Yankee land, but they have a Texas attitude.

Chapter Fifteen

The Early Teal Season

As a swollen sun peeked over the horizon, a familiar whistle tickled my eardrums. Seconds later, a flock of blue-winged teal buzzed our boat at breakneck speed. It was a sight my hunting partner and I had seen hundreds of times, but this one caught us by surprise.

The shock came not from the birds' incredible swiftness or daredevil navigation, but from the fact that we were on Lake Guri in a remote corner of the Venezuelan rainforest. Six weeks earlier, we had hunted these birds on the upper Texas coast, and now they were among parrots, howler monkeys, and anacondas in South America.

Bluewings migrate in September, giving hunters an early crack at waterfowl hunting action. The season follows their southward movement, which can be intense. At the first hint of a cold front, bluewings quickly exit our borders and head toward the tropics.

Fortunately, Texas hunters have plenty of opportunities to hunt them on public land while they are here. The key to success is learning what makes these pint-sized ducks tick and applying that knowledge to scouting their habitat.

The most important factor in having a successful teal hunt is finding an area with the right water supply. Dry marshes and fields send teal south quickly, while too much water spreads them out so much that hunters have a difficult time luring them into shotgun range.

The author considers blue-winged teal to be one of the most beautiful ducks in North America. They are fast flying and have the tastiest of flesh.

The 2002-2003 season was prime example. Jacob Virdine, who works at the J.D. Murphree Wildlife Management Area near Port Arthur, said 49 hunters showed up there for opening day. Those hunters shot only 48 teal. The next day, 35 hunters took two dozen birds.

"The problem was our water level was too deep for teal," Virdine said. It was just right a couple of days before the opener, but then it rained really hard."

The same storm system dropped only a couple of inches of rain in the rice fields to the west, which produced limits of teal for hunters during opening weekend.

Back in 1998, the Texas coast experienced a brutal summer-long drought. Two days before teal season opened, Tropical Storm Frances hit, dumping water everywhere on the coast. Instead of shooting in marshes, hunters were shooting teal out of flooded cattle pastures where the birds had easier feeding on floating seed.

Since hunters cannot control the rain, how should they prepare for early teal season? The key is scouting, said Anahuac National Wildlife Refuge (NWR) Manager Kelly McDowell: "Many of our hunters are first-timers from the Houston area, and lots of times, hectic schedules and such do not allow them any time to scout. Sometimes there are so many birds it does not matter much, but other times they will discover too much water or not enough water. Scouting is the key to successful hunting, especially on public land."

McDowell is right. Because of scouting efforts, I have been able to bag teal on public lands when others had a tough time.

Teal are dabbling ducks and thus prefer shallow mud flats and grass beds in marshes where they eat milfoil, seeds of pond weeds, and tiny mollusks. High water can cover areas that would normally be productive, but knowing the topography of the land and locating higher ground that might hold only a few inches of water can yield results.

In the Lower Neches Wildlife Management Area near Bridge City, I go to an island that has a shallow pond in the middle of it. Tropical storm-level tides make it about 6 inches deep, and a magnet for teal during periods of high and low water. It seems to be better during high tides because the birds can see the vegetation more easily than in the foot-deep water around it.

With the advent of the internet, scouting is no longer confined to physically exploring hunting areas. Websites such as topozone.com provide

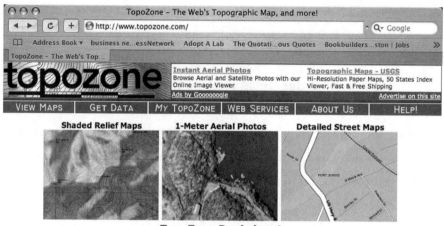

topozone.com

detailed topographical maps of any location in the United States and can help you pick out spots that would hold water and be potential ambush spots for teal.

I had passed by the island described above dozens of times, but after studying the area on the internet, I found the little pond and a true teal-hunting hotspot.

Teal are small and offer a challenging target, but they are easy to hunt during the September season. They are creatures of habit, so you can generally count on them to feed both early and late.

The first thing to consider is setting up a blind. In the case of teal, this does not require a lot of effort. Teal are certainly not blind-shy during the early season, so hunting out of a boat draped in camouflage netting or covered by roseau cane is more than adequate. Or you can simply wear plenty of camouflage and sit still.

For years, hunters brought dozens of decoys for the early season, but that is becoming outdated. A dozen decoys of any kind of duck set out in the marsh will give these sociable birds an inviting place to land and you a place to shoot.

I usually bring only half a dozen teal decoys, a few shoveler imitations, and a mechanical decoy, and have no problem scoring limits of teal. Sometimes I use a "confidence" decoy such as a great blue heron, a common sight on the Texas coast and most freshwater reservoirs in September.

Calling teal is rather simple, although many hunters on public lands tend to overdo it. Simple teal whistles sounded a few times at the sight of birds is enough to lure them. Too much calling spooks them. I have been in areas where hunters a few ponds away called too much and pushed birds right to me.

Part of a successful hunt on public land is using the mistakes of other hunters to your advantage. It seems there is always someone who calls too much, shoots when the birds are too high, or arrives in the field late and pushes birds to you. This might be frustrating, but if you keep your cool, you should get a shot at some of "their" birds.

When you do get a shot, make sure not to use a heavy load, which can destroy the meat in the tiny breasts. I use No. 6, but 7-1/2 will work as well.

Improved cylinder or modified chokes work great for teal, especially in close quarters. These are incredibly fast birds that can fly at 60 miles an hour. Make sure to lead them by at least 5 feet when they are 20 yards away, and double that when they are out past 30 yards.

Making a paper-cutting sound as they move, teal seem to come out of nowhere. I do not know how many times I have thought nothing was going to happen and then a flock of bluewings lands right in the decoys. Once a small flock buzzed right over me and landed less than 10 feet from my blind. The encounter excited me so much, I never thought to shoot until my partner's hyperactive dog alerted them and sent them packing.

Some hunters might consider that a failure, but I consider it the ultimate success. The day I quit being in awe of nature is the day I put away my decoys for good. With their super-fast flight and rapid migration, blue-winged teal remind us that good things come and go quickly, but the memory stays with us forever.

BEWARE OF ALLIGATORS

Because teal season occurs when temperatures are plenty warm enough for alligators and snakes to prowl, pay special attention to your dogs. There are thousands of gators in Texas marshes, and they would love nothing more than to get hold of your hunting partner.

PHOTO COURTESY OF THE U.S. FISH AND WILDLIFE SERVICE

Alligators are a potentially big threat to dogs on duck hunts, particularly in the early teal season. Their numbers have skyrocketed in Texas to the point of being arguably overpopulated.

Mark Hall of Central Flyway Outfitters in Winnie recalled the narrow escape of his beloved retriever:

"She ran out toward the reservoir behind the lodge, and when she came back after a while, I noticed she was walking funny, so I went over to her. She was a bloody mess, and I figured there was no way she was going to live. It was obvious a gator had attacked her.

"When I tried to pick her up, it put her in terrible pain because her hips were in bad, bad shape. The car was 100 yards or so off, and she followed me all the way with messed up hips and teeth marks all over. She then hopped up in the pet porter like she always did and rode to the vet without a complaint."

After extensive surgery, the dog recovered and returned to the marsh to hunt again.

"After my dog narrowly escaped a big alligator, I now refuse to bring a dog into the marshes I hunt during September. You might not want to go that far, but you should be mindful of the danger," Hall said.

Chapter Sixteen

Duck Recipes:
So, I killed this duck—now what?

I am always amazed at the number of times people ask me: "What do you do with the ducks and geese you shoot?"

If that question were about speckled trout or deer, chances are whoever asked would be vying for some free meat. However, with waterfowl, most people think they are worthless on the table, tasting like a combination of mud, fish, and grass at best. These people could not be more wrong.

I personally love to eat duck, and not just in gumbos or stew in which a hippo hoof would probably taste good. Duck and goose are very good in a variety of recipes, of which I will share a few shortly. If you want to eat just chicken, beef, and pork the rest of your life, go ahead; I personally prefer diversity in my diet, and love to eat the stuff I kill.

Before we go into how to prepare these delicious birds, there are some things to consider.

The first would be which ducks and geese are good to eat. This is a matter of personal taste. I know people who love to eat ducks that others

Some hunters dislike the flavor of snow geese, but the author finds they taste just fine if prepared right. His favorite way to cook them is by chicken frying the breast meat. Long-time guide Harlan Hatcher got him started on his love for fried snow goose years ago.

frown upon. The general rule is that puddle ducks are the best and divers are the least tasty. That stands to reason, as puddle ducks eat more vegetation, while divers eat fish, crustaceans, and other invertebrates. While conducting research for this chapter, I came across a poll that Delta Waterfowl did among their staff as to which ducks were culinary favorites, least favorites, and the most under- and overrated. It was pretty interesting:

Delta staffer Mike Nevins listed coot (not technically a duck but close enough) as his favorite, followed closely by blue-winged teal. The least favorite was merganser. He could find no overrated species and felt coot was the most underrated.

John Devney picked blue-winged teal as the favorite, green-winged as second, goldeneye as least favorite, gadwall most overrated, and ringneck underrated.

Jim Fisher picked canvasback as his favorite, mallard second, scoter least favorite, mallard most overrated, and scaup as underrated.

Ken Richkus picked wood duck as his favorite, green-winged teal second favorite, merganser as least favorite, mallard as most overrated, and widgeon as most underrated.

Joel Brice named blue-winged teal his favorite followed by mallard, bufflehead as the worst, mallard as most overrated, and shoveler as underrated.

Delta Director Rob Olson picked mallard as his favorite, blue-winged teal as second, merganser as worst, canvasback as most overrated, and ringneck as most underrated.

Blue-winged teal ended up the most often selected favorite, with ring-

Blue-winged teal is hard to beat in the taste department. It is just a shame they are so small. There is not much more meat than on a dove.

neck as most underrated and, surprisingly, mallard as the most overrated. Again, it is all personal taste.

My list is wood duck as my favorite, blue-winged teal a close second, merganser as the worst (they just plain suck), mallard as the most overrated,

A good pair of shears like these made by Gerber go a long way in helping to clean and prepare ducks and geese. For those who simply like to breast them out, all you have to do is pull the skin away from the breast, cut down the sides of the ribs, snip off the wings and a few tendons, and you are done.

and most underrated without a doubt—ringneck. I love eating ringneck. Shoveler are a close second in that department. Most of the time they taste just fine, especially if they have been eating rice. Mallard are good, but to me no better than pintail, gadwall, or widgeon.

As far as geese go, there is no question in my mind: specklebelly is best. In fact, I prefer eating specklebelly to wood duck, and that says something because I flat out get wood duck cravings. The flavor of most other geese such as snow, Ross', and Canada depends on

what they have been eating. I find that if you marinate any goose and chicken-fry it, it turns out great.

A big part of making sure that your waterfowl taste good on the table is field handling. The Clemson University Extension Service has an awesome instruction manual for field dressing birds. It goes as follows:

- Remove the entrails and crop as soon as possible, because the grain in the crop might ferment if not removed.
- The heart and liver may be saved for giblets. Store in a plastic bag on ice to keep them clean and cold.

- Leave an identification mark on the bird as required by state game regulations.
- The birds may be plucked or skinned in the field. If you pluck the birds, bring a plastic bag for storing the feathers.
- Cool the carcass quickly to retain flavor and maintain the quality of the bird. A temperature above 40 degrees Fahrenheit is meat's worst enemy.
- Wipe out the cavity with a clean cloth or paper towel. Do not use grass or snow, as this will contaminate the carcass.
- Allow air to circulate in the carcass by hanging or laying the bird in a well-ventilated place.
- In hot weather, place the birds individually in plastic bags and put on ice.
- Do not pile warm birds in a mass.
- Store birds in a cooler on ice out of the sun.

The Clemson tips included a note that it is important to keep birds cool during transport from the field to home: "The best way to store birds is in a cooler on ice. If this is not possible, keep the car well ventilated and put the birds on the back seat or the floor. Do not transport them in the trunk because the enclosed space does not allow heat to escape from the birds."

If you do not do all of this, do not feel bad. I do not either, but these are good guidelines, and the more effort you take to keep your birds in good condition, the better they will taste.

BIRD FLU

Some have raised concerns about contracting bird flu after handling infected birds. Although the likelihood is low, Ducks Unlimited encourages hunters to heed the standard precautions offered by the U.S. Geological Survey National Wildlife Health Center for protecting themselves against any wildlife related diseases. There is always a low probability of transmission when handling infected harvested animals:

- Do not handle birds that are obviously sick or found dead.
- Keep your game birds cool, clean, and dry.
- Do not eat, drink, or smoke while cleaning your birds.
- Use disposable, surgical gloves when cleaning game, and properly dispose of them when done.
- Wash your hands with soap and water or alcohol wipes after dressing birds.
- Clean all tools and surfaces immediately afterwards. Use hot soapy water, then disinfect with a 10 percent chlorine bleach solution.

Is it ok to eat ducks?

Yes, according to DU and every other organization involved with waterfowl and human health at the time of this writing. DU notes that the standard recommendation for ensuring that any wild game is safely cooked is to cook all types of meat thoroughly (155 to 165 degrees internal temperature) to kill disease organisms and parasites.

PHOTOS BY HUGO PEDRAZA

Chef Lester Binnick graduated from the Culinary Institute of America (CIA) January 1981. He is a Certified Executive Chef in the American Culinary Federation. He serves as Executive Chef at Houston's most exclusive private country clubs, and has prepared foods for U.S. presidents and other dignitaries. **New York Times, Newsday,** *and the* **Houston Post** *have given glowing reviews to restaurants where he served as Executive Chef.*

RECIPES

Duck Breast with Balsamic Butter Sauce & Parsnip Grits

(Chef Lester Binnick, CEC)

Makes 6 Servings

Marinade

6 each Duck Breast Filets scored

2 each shallots minced

1 tsp allspice ground

1 tsp cloves ground

1 1/2 teaspoons coriander ground

2 tsp cumin ground

2 oz. olive oil

1/2 tsp salt

1/2 tsp black pepper ground

Balsamic Butter Sauce:

1 oz. butter unsalted

1/2 lb. shallots chopped

6 oz. white wine

2 oz. rosemary sprigs fresh chopped

12 oz. balsamic vinegar

2 1/2 oz. butter unsalted diced

Parsnip Grits:

1/2 lb. parsnips peeled and sliced

1/2 cup quick grits

2 cups water

1/8 tsp. salt

Marinade:

Score duck breast skin at 1/2 inch intervals. Rotate duck breast and score again making a criss cross pattern. Combine next 8 ingredients, mix well and pour over duck breasts. Coat well and marinate covered in refrigerator at least one hour.

Remove duck from marinade. Heat pan. Cook breasts skin side down approximately 14 minutes until skin is crisp and brown. Turn breast over and cook 4 more minutes. Finish cooking in a 350° oven at 6 minutes or until internal temperature reaches 160° F. Cool duck 5 minutes before slicing.

PHOTOS BY HUGO PEDRAZA

Balsamic Butter Sauce:

Saute shallots in 1 oz. of butter until soft. Add white wine, rosemary and balsamic vinegar. Simmer until liquid is reduced by 3/4. Strain and put back into pot and heat. Using a wire whip, add butter to the reduced vinegar while whipping adding the butter little by little until melted and all is incorporated. DO NOT BOIL.

Parsnip Grits

Boil parsnips in water until soft. Drain. Sift through a wire mesh strainer to remove any fibrous strands. Bring water and salt to a rolling boil. Slowly stir in grits; reduce to low heat. Cook 5 to 7 minutes; stirring frequently. Remove from heat; cover; let stand until thickened; stir. Place parsnip and grits in food processor. Puree. Place Parsnip grits in center of warm plate. Slice duck on a 45 degree angle and place on top of mix. Drizzle sauce around and on duck.

Per serving (excluding unknown items): 169.3 Calories: 9.8 Fat (54.2 Calories from fat); 16 Protein; 17.1 Carbohydrate; 0 Cholesterol; 237 Sodium.

Chicken Fried Duck or Goose

Duck or goose breast, no skin or bones (approx. two per person for duck, one for geese)

milk
eggs
flour
garlic, salt, pepper, Cajun seasonings of choice
vegetable oil

Make sure that all shot is removed from meat. Cut duck into bite-sized pieces and cover with milk. Allow the meat to soak in milk for at least an hour in refrigerator.

Put a cup of flour on a plate and season with garlic, salt, and pepper, or your favorite seasoning to taste. Amount of flour depends on amount of duck; adjust accordingly. In a small bowl, make a mixture of one cup milk and one egg. Dip breasts in milk and egg then roll in the flour to cover meat with flour.

Heat oil in deep frying pan to 350 degrees. Carefully place breaded duck in oil and fry until golden brown. Remove from oil and place on paper towels to allow oil to drain. Salt immediately. Serve with peppered white gravy.

All Day Duck

2 ducks, cut into serving pieces

1 medium onion, chopped

2 cloves garlic, chopped

1 cup white wine or chicken broth (low sodium)

1 green bell pepper, chopped

1 ripe tomato, seeded and chopped

salt, pepper

Season the duck to taste. Arrange duck in the bottom of crock pot, top with remaining ingredients. Cook on low for six to eight hours or until duck is tender. Serve with rice and steamed vegetables

Jalapeño Duck or Goose Bites

10 jalapeño peppers, halved and seeded

cubed cheese, preferably cheddar

duck or goose meat cut in thin strips 1-inch wide, 1/4-inch thick

bacon

toothpicks

Fill peppers with cheese. Wrap duck or goose on top of cheese and wrap half strip of bacon around all. Stick toothpick through all ingredients and grill until done. Can also be baked or broiled in oven. Make sure bacon is cooked thoroughly. Serve with Ranch or blue cheese dressing as a dipping sauce.

Duck with Pecan Stuffing

2 large ducks, cleaned

4 cups soft breadcrumbs

1 cup finely chopped onion

1 cup pecans, chopped

1/2 cup milk, scalded

1 cup finely chopped celery

1 cup seedless raisins

1/2 teaspoon salt

2 eggs, beaten

6 slices bacon

1/4 cup Worcestershire sauce

1 cup ketchup

1/4 cup steak sauce

1/2 cup chili sauce

Mix breadcrumbs, celery, onions, raisins, nuts, and salt together. Add hot milk to the beaten eggs and then add to dry mixture.

Place ducks in roasting pan and fill with stuffing. Place in roaster and cover each duck with three strips of bacon. Roast uncovered in oven at 350 degrees, allowing 15 to 20 minutes per pound. Combine the last four ingredients and baste the ducks with the sauce during the last 20 minutes of cooking. Remove ducks to serving platter. Skim fat from the sauce and serve with the ducks.

Parmesan Duck Breast

2 duck breasts, boned, sliced thin

1/4 cup parmesan cheese

1 egg, beaten mixed with 1 teaspoon water

1 cup vegetable oil

Heat oil in heavy skillet. Dip pieces of duck breast in beaten egg and roll in Parmesan cheese. Fry in hot oil until done. Serve with pasta and garlic bread.

Baked Duck in Sweet and Sour Sauce

2 wild ducks

1 orange, sliced

1 apple, sliced

2 tablespoon oil

2 tablespoons brown sugar

1/4 cup Worcestershire sauce

3/4 cup ketchup

2 tablespoon lemon juice

1/2 cup onion, grated

1/2 teaspoon paprika

1/4 cup white vinegar

Rinse the ducks and pat dry inside and out, then stuff with sliced fruit. Rub the outside with oil and place in a baking dish. Combine the remaining ingredients in a bowl, mixing well, and spoon over the ducks. Cover tightly with foil and bake in a 325-degree oven for two hours or until tender, then uncover and bake until browned.

Duck A L'Orange

2 ducks, cleaned and dried

bacon, 6 slices

6 ounces frozen orange juice thawed

Barrows

C/9

Black Bellied Whistling Duck

Cinnamon Teal

American Coot

Fulvous Whistling Duck

Lesser Scaup

Mottled Duck

Ross' Goose

White-fronted Goose

3/4 teaspoon mustard

1/2 teaspoon salt

1 cup water

Season ducks with salt and pepper, and place in roasting pan breast sides up. Cover with strips of bacon. Roast at 400 degrees for 25 minutes or until done to taste.

In small saucepan, heat the orange juice, garlic, mustard, and salt to a boil. Remove from heat. During the last 10 minutes, remove bacon from ducks and brush them with the mixture. Thicken orange sauce with cornstarch mixed with 1/4 cup of water. Pour in remaining water and stir over low heat until sauce thickens. Place ducks on heated platter, slice, and serve with the orange sauce.

Barbecued Duck

2 cleaned wild ducks

1 bottle BBQ sauce of choice

Place ducks in a 13x9-inch baking dish. Preheat oven to 350 degrees. Bake ducks for 1-1/2 to 2 hours until tender. Heat sauce in a small saucepan and baste duck with sauce during the last 30 minutes of cooking.

Duck and Sausage Gumbo

1 cup cooking oil

1/2 cup flour

1 cup onion, chopped

1/4 cup green onions, chopped

3 quarts boiling water

Tabasco sauce

salt

cayenne pepper

2 large duck breasts, sliced

1/4 cup parsley, chopped

1/2 cup green onion tops, chopped

2 cloves garlic, diced

1/2 pound smoked sausage, sliced

2 cups cooked rice

Heat 1/2 cup of the oil over medium heat in a large heavy pot. Add the flour, stirring constantly with a whisk until dark brown. Add the onion and green onion and cook until tender in the roux. Add the boiling water and season with Tabasco, salt, and cayenne pepper.

Season the duck with salt and red pepper. Sauté the duck pieces in a skillet with remaining oil. Add cooked duck to gumbo. Allow gumbo to simmer uncovered for three hours. During the last 30 minutes of cooking, add sausage, green onion tops, garlic, and parsley. Serve over rice with gumbo file.

Duck and Sausage Gumbo
(The Lisa Moore Busy Cook Version)

1 bell pepper, chopped

1 large onion, chopped

3 ribs celery, chopped

1/4 teaspoon garlic, minced

10 cups cool water

1 cup instant roux mix (Tony Chachere's)

2-3 pounds duck or goose pieces

1/2 pound smoked sausage, sliced

Creole seasoning to taste

green onions, sliced

In a stockpot coated with cooking spray, sauté vegetables until soft. In the same pot, prepare roux mix according to directions on package. Add remaining water and meat, bring to a boil, and reduce to a simmer. Continue cooking until meat is tender. Season gumbo to taste with Creole seasoning. Serve gumbo over steamed rice and top with green onions and gumbo file.

Rosemary and Apricot Duck

3 tablespoon chopped fresh rosemary

2 tablespoons brown sugar

1 tablespoon black pepper

2 teaspoons salt

4 (3/4-pound) duck breasts, skinned and halved

1 tablespoon olive oil

1/2 cup sugar

1/2 cup champagne or white wine vinegar

5 apricots, quartered

Combine the rosemary, brown sugar, black pepper, and salt. Rub the mixture over the duck breasts. Cover and chill two hours. Rinse duck with cold water, pat dry.

Heat olive oil in a large nonstick skillet over medium-high heat. Add duck and cook for five minutes on each side or until done. Remove from pan. Let stand for 10 minutes.

Combine the sugar and vinegar in a small saucepan, and bring to a boil. Cook until thick and amber-colored (about five minutes). Add apricots, reduce heat, and cook for one minute or until the apricots begin to soften.

Cut duck diagonally across the grain into slices and serve with caramelized apricots.

Duck Jambalaya

1 package jambalaya rice mix

1 cup celery, diced

1/2 cup onion, chopped

2 medium tomatoes, chopped

2 pounds duck or goose pieces

2 tablespoon oil

1/2 cup flour

Dust duck pieces in flour. In a hot skillet with oil, brown duck on all sides and set aside.

Prepare jambalaya rice according to package directions. Pour into a deep baking dish. Place duck on top of rice. Sprinkle top with celery, onions, and tomatoes. Cover tightly. Bake in a preheated 375-degree oven for one hour. Remove from oven. Let sit covered five minutes. Remove foil and serve.

Baked Wild Duck in Oven Bag

1-2 ducks

melted butter

seasonings

chopped apple and celery

1 tablespoon flour

1 cup orange juice

Preheat oven to 350 degrees. Place small or medium oven bag in 2-inch deep roasting pan. Mix orange juice and flour until well mixed, then pour into bag. Brush duck with butter and season cavity and outside. Fill cavity with chopped apple and celery. Place duck in bag. Close bag with twist tie and make six 1/2-inch slits in top. Cook 1-1/2 hours.

Roasted Wild Duck

2 ducks

1/4 teaspoon salt

1/4 teaspoon pepper

1 cup onion, chopped

1 cup apple, diced

1 cup celery, diced

1 teaspoon garlic

11 ounces beef broth or consommé

1 cup red wine

2 teaspoons Worcestershire sauce

Season ducks inside and out with salt and pepper. Combine onions, apples, celery, and garlic. Mix well and stuff ducks loosely with the onion mixture. Truss legs and wingtips with cotton twine. Place breast down into a roasting pan. Pour consommé and wine over the top, then sprinkle Worcestershire sauce over all of it. Roast at 325 degrees for three hours, basting often. Turn breast side up and continue cooking for 30-60 minutes until browned, basting often. Serve hot

Great Grilled Duck

8 duck breast filets

2 tablespoons finely minced fresh rosemary leaves

1 tablespoon finely minced fresh thyme

2 large cloves of garlic finely minced

fresh ground black pepper

Soak duck breasts in a brine solution overnight. Remove breasts and rinse, then grind fresh black pepper over both sides. Add extra pepper if you prefer your duck spicy. Rub the minced spices thoroughly over both sides of the breasts and let sit for an hour. Grill to desired doneness (we prefer medium-rare at our house). Slice the breasts into thin strips across the grain and serve with a rice or potato side dish. A hearty red wine goes well.

MARINATING MEAT

Marinating any kind of meat helps the taste, and this is especially true for the diving ducks. I like to marinate in wine, buttermilk, or limejuice. Another good marinade is any kind of standard cola, as the acid will draw out any funky taste. My wife Lisa and I generally marinate our duck just an hour before cooking, and it always comes out tasting great.

SELECTING & PREPARING BIRDS FOR TAXIDERMY

Almost as cool as eating ducks and geese is getting them mounted. I am a taxidermy nut—always have been, always will be. My house looks like a wildlife and fisheries museum, and the office I am sitting in typing this chapter is slowly becoming the Chester Moore Waterfowl Wing. You know that anyone who has an alligator garfish mounted attacking a blue-winged teal is serious about having dead stuff in his house.

Once again, picking which duck or goose you want to mount is a personal choice. It might be your first duck, or the first of a particular kind. It might be one that you shot on a special hunt. Do not listen to people who say, "Don't mount that bird because it's not a mallard" or pintail, or whatever kind of "glory" bird they are into. These people are generally idiots.

There are a few guidelines for choosing birds if you want maximum bang for your buck. First off, the bird must be in good condition. If you bring in the prettiest duck in the world and it looks as if it was run over by an 18-wheeler, there is not a whole lot a taxidermist can do with it. Some taxidermists can do wonders, but they cannot work miracles.

The author combined this alligator gar head mount with a blue-winged teal he shot the same year to make a unique predator-prey mount. He now has plans for a mink attacking a mottled duck hen on the nest.

The best-looking specimens are mature, fully feathered ones with lots of color and all the right plumage for the particular species. The best-looking pintail drakes, for example, have a big sprigtail and long neck. Big, mature mallard drakes with prominently curled tail feathers are tops for that species, and a specklebelly with a bunch of bars on the chest looks great.

What it boils down to is that the best looking are those with the markings you see in field guides. Unfortunately, some species are hard to get that

Taxidermist Bubba Andres of Winnie puts the finishing touches on a pair of albino shovelers. Such "freak" specimens are popular with hunters that have a taxidermy fixation.

way, as they get into full plumage mainly after the season is over. Blue-winged teal are a fine example. I have been fortunate enough to shoot only one in full plumage, and it was during the last week of the season back in 1999. It is currently mounted in a flying position over my entertainment center.

If you want to get a duck or goose mounted, take extra special care to keep it in good shape. Get it away from the retriever as soon as possible. In fact, if you know it is a duck you want to mount, hold the dog off and get it yourself if possible. I know that good retrievers are not supposed to mess anything up, but it happens. Keep the specimen cool, dry, and clean. Wrap it in paper towels or newspaper, and if you cannot make it to a taxidermist quickly, put it in the freezer. Do your best to keep blood off the feathers, as it will sometimes leave irremovable stains.

My goal is to have one of each kind of waterfowl species in North and South America mounted. At the time of this writing, I have a huge mallard drake, canvasback, a pair of bufflehead, and a specklebelly at my taxidermist, Sonny Carlin. I have this striking feeling that he will be getting more business next season, and the next, and the next....

Chapter
Seventeen

Adventures in Waterfowling

The concept seemed simple: Crawl on our bellies up to a levee, slow-ly creep over the top, click off our safeties, and commence to firing at the hun-dreds of snow geese chowing down on the rye grass on the other side.

My partner for this trip, Jacob Curtis of Houston, and I just knew that on this late February morning our electronic calls would produce a bunch of geese. However, the fog we had anticipated never showed up and here we were crawling on our bellies toward these geese that wanted nothing to do with our decoys and seemed to have a crack-head-like addiction to the rye grass.

I like "creeping," as it is commonly called. It reminds me of when all of the neighborhood boys would play war on the weekend, and my buddy, Chris, and I would crawl through this big ditch down the street from our house to ambush our buddies at their hideout.

The crawl was going well. I mean it was going as well as any trip on your belly through mud, slime, cattle manure, and goose feathers could be. Just as we passed the tenth manure pile, I figured we had about 30 more yards to go. I signaled Jacob to split off to the left so he could position himself next to some bushes at the top of the levee. His gun shot only 3-inch shells, and there was a cluster of geese just on the other side of the bushes. My gun shot 3-1/2s, so I would tackle the geese that were a little farther out.

He headed his way and I headed mine until I came across a little problem. Well, actually it was a pretty big problem, at least from the perspective of someone on their belly. Right in my line of crawling was a nutria.

I kept hearing something splashing in the water as we crawled, but I figured it was an ibis or egret. Apparently, it was this nutria, which had crossed in front of me, turned around, and had its beady eyes fixed on Yours Truly.

Any other time I would have greeted the ugly rat with some steel shot, but that would spook the geese and I would feel like even more of a jackass for crawling on my belly in this sludge.

This nutria obviously wasn't the most intelligent of its kind because it started walking toward me. I started crawling to the right to avoid the pesky varmint, but it was intent on following me. Now I was getting worried. Maybe this thing was rabid or something, because it sure wasn't acting normally.

With nothing but a 30-pound rat standing between me and a bunch of snow geese, I grabbed a shell out of my pocket, rose to my knees, and made a pitch that would make Nolan Ryan proud. I hit the rat square in the head. At first, the stupid thing didn't move, but then as if a light bulb went off over its head, the rat barreled off toward the levee.

My thoughts were that with my luck that morning, it would probably hop over the levee, scare the geese, and screw up our plan. And that's exactly what happened. Well, sort of.

Jacob was already in position, so when the geese jumped up, he fired and took down half a dozen. Some of the geese flew right over me in their horror at the orange-toothed rodent running at them, and I managed to get two of them, so it wasn't a total loss.

PHOTO COURTESY OF THE U.S. FISH AND WILDLIFE SERVICE

Nutria are huge rodents imported from South America years ago, and are now present throughout much of Texas. They are major pests, out-competing native muskrats for food, making holes in levees, and getting in the way of the author while goose hunting.

The next time however, I'll just shoot the rat and worry about the geese later.

That story is just one example of the many funny and exciting things I have experienced hunting waterfowl around the country. I wanted to share some of them with you, because I know there is one thing waterfowlers like almost as much as hunting, and that is telling stories about hunting.

One of the funniest things that ever happened to me was during the opening day of the 2000 season. Outdoor writer Larry Bozka and I were hunting with Will Beaty's Central Flyway Outfitters, and we had a big wad of teal show up right at first shooting light.

There were 10 hunters in pit blinds along the levee where we were hunting, and the 20 or so birds didn't have much of a chance if we were even half good shots. Bozka and I fired away at three birds that were on our end of the setup, and after dispensing all six of our rounds, the birds fell. The last one we shot at must have decided it was going to go out in a blaze of glory and take out a hunter, because it started spiraling toward us at immense speed.

Larry and I looked on in horror as this teal headed straight for us with the last bit of strength it had. (When you are in a pit blind, there is no real way to retreat or even duck for that matter.) I knew it wouldn't kill us, but a duck traveling at the speed it was could easily break a nose or crack a rib, and that would be hard to explain back home. "Honey, I need to go to the hospital, a green-winged teal gave me one hell of a rib shot this morning."

Oddly, that would probably pass muster in my household, as my wife is used to that kind of thing by now. Nonetheless, the prospects of getting hit by a kamikaze teal were not very thrilling.

Larry and I looked at each other with that "Oh, well" look and watched as the seemingly angry teal hit the ground,

Teal certainly do not seem dangerous when in the jaws of a lab, but when they are flying at you at 50 miles per hour, you might think differently.

literally lodging itself in the 4- to 5-inch gap between our blinds. We got revenge by our group bagging about 40 of its relatives that morning and putting that one in a gumbo back at camp.

That same year, I got to hunt with 1996 Olympic trap shooting champion Kim Rhode. This lovely young lady was helping Beaty out with a youth hunting project at the Anahuac National Wildlife Refuge that weekend, and I was fortunate enough to get to share a blind with her on an awesome slough north of Winnie the morning before the event.

It was a perfect duck day, with overcast sky mixed with rain all morning that kept the ducks moving in a big way. There were five of us in the blind that morning, including our guide, Harlan Hatcher, who after we took a few shots, said, "I don't know why we're even bothering. Kim is just wearing them out."

And she was.

I kid you not when I say she was shooting ringnecks that that were flying from right to left of the blind at a good speed at 40 and 45 yards. She was almost at a limit before the rest of us had a duck or two apiece. Finally, a mottled duck swung low at about 30 yards and the Olympic champion missed. This, of course, was the opportunity the rest of us had been waiting for, so we could give her a hard time.

"It's good to see a gold medalist can miss," I jokingly said to her.

Without blinking, she said, "No, I was just trying to make you guys feel better."

We all had a good laugh and the rest of us realized we were in the presence of a true class act.

Back when I was in high school, the gully down the street from my house was loaded with wood ducks in the winter. We lived in the city limits of West Orange, so firing a shotgun was not allowed. There were no provisions, however, against shooting a bow, and I figured that I could sneak up in the thick woods along the gully, jump up the ducks, and fire amongst them with a judo point and bring down a duck or two. This was not one of my more ingenious ideas.

After school one day, I drove by the gully and saw half a dozen woodies swimming out near the road. I knew the rest must be back around the bend where they usually hung out. I quickly went home, grabbed my Martin Tiger bow along with two arrows fixed with judo points, and headed back toward the gully. It took me about 10 minutes once I hit the woods to creep down toward the bend where the ducks were hanging out—and there was no doubt they were there. Those woodies were carrying on as if throwing a party.

There was a little clearing right past this big cypress tree, and I figured if I could get up to it, I could ease around the side, draw back, the ducks would jump off, and my arrow would connect with one of them.

It sounded good, anyway. That is, until about 30 yards from the tree, I noticed a pair of woodies feeding on acorns right in front of me. I tried to remain still, but the red-eyed drake spotted me, signaling his hen that it was time to go and letting out a whistle that told the rest of the ducks there was some idiot out here with a bow and arrow. They all jumped up from the gully and headed north on the west bank. I figured nothing from nothing leaves nothing, so I drew back my bow and fired a Hail Mary shot toward them, but it never connected.

That was my first and only attempt at killing ducks with a bow.

Back in January 2005, I visited my friends, Hallie and Jerome Metzger, at their home in Palo Cedro, California, which is right on the edge of the Sierra Nevada range. Hallie and I are like brother and sister, and we both share a passion for whacking things, particularly waterfowl.

Jerome used to guide for Canada geese in the mountains, so on my visit they took me up for a hunt. They told me to dress in layers because it would be really cold early and heat up as the day wore on. I got out of the truck in the 7-degree temperatures, standing in 3 feet of snow looking like the Michelin Man from the television commercials. Hallie said I looked like a tick that was ready to bust, but I was warm and that was all that mattered to me.

We had a ways to walk to set up our decoys and lay down blinds, so

I grabbed a couple of bags and started walking. Well, I walked about 50 yards and fell on my face. For a moment, I felt like the little kid in *A Christmas Story* that falls in the snow and could not get up because he had so many clothes on. I writhed around like a turtle on its back for a minute or so before I got to my feet and headed toward my partners.

Jerome was about 50 yards ahead, but Hallie was a good 100 yards in front of me and showing no signs of slowing down. I pride myself on staying in good shape, but I learned quickly that my workouts pale in comparison to walking in thick snow. I think I lost two pant sizes that morning.

The hunting was slow that morning, but we did manage to get a couple of Canadas. What was amazing to me is just how cold it was. Hallie's hair frosted before we set up the decoys. I vowed to never complain about Texas winters again. You hear a lot of gibberish from people around here going, "It's a dry cold out West." Bull cookies. Cold is cold, and this Texas boy froze his natural born ass off in pursuit of geese that were apparently smarter than we were. There weren't many of them around in this winter wonderland.

As the mist that had hung around all morning subsided, I looked back toward the barn where we parked, and realized it was only about 300 yards away. I honestly thought we had walked a good 3/4

The author's friend, Hallie Metzger, goofs around with a Canada goose bagged in the mountains of northern California. She was dressed in half the clothes he was, but did not get as cold. So much for dressing in layers!

PHOTO BY JEROME METZGER

The author looks like a cross between a yeti (complete with a sagital crest-looking beanie) as he and Hallie Metzger pose with this Canada goose. As you can see, this environment is too cold for rational waterfowlers.

of a mile. I had a ball that morning with my friends in the beautiful environment, but was flat cold and worn out.

On our way home, my kind hosts asked what I thought about my first hunt for geese in the snowy mountains of California.

My reply?

"Thank God for Texas."

Chapter Eighteen

For the Dogs

I love dogs, always have, and always will. Over the years, I have owned a number of them, ranging from shih-tzu to German shepherds, mutts, and Labradors, but I have never owned a good hunting retriever. That is somewhat ironic since I spend so much time pursuing waterfowl, but I have always done my own retrieving or used my friends' retrievers. Outdoor writer Larry Bozka used to call me the "Chesamo Retriever," as I was usually the one on our hunts that would walk through the mud to get whatever ducks

A good hunting retriever makes life much easier on a hunter, and a lot more enjoyable. There is no more loyal friend than a duck and goose dog.

and geese we shot.

My good friend Hallie Metzger of Palo Cedro, California, raises Chesapeake Bay retrievers, and when her dog Delta had pups in February of 2006, she offered me pick of the litter. I could not refuse. Chesapeakes, or "Chessies," as hunters frequently call them, are not popular in our region and sort of have a bad reputation as being "independent," to say the least. Hallie's line of dogs has always been friendly, and great hunters as Hallie and her husband Jerome frequently hunt ducks and Canada geese near their home with their Chessies. Hunters buy up their pups like hotcakes.

PHOTO BY LISA MOORE

The author watches Tarja make her first-ever retrieve in a pond on his friend's property in Orange County.

One thing no one can deny about Chessies is that they are incredibly strong swimmers. Breeders created the breed to hunt on big, deep water, and they have saved more people from drowning than any other breed.

I like to hunt the open bays, reservoirs, and even the surf from time to time, so I figured a Chessie would be good for me.

A few weeks ago, I flew out to California to get my dog and bring it back home. The bonus was I got to visit with my friends, which is something my wife and I try to do a couple of times a year. When I got there, I met my puppy, which I immediately named Tarja (tar-ya). Yes, I know it is an unusual name, but for years, I named all of my dogs after female wrestlers, and there are none out there now that I currently would like to name my dog after.

I really like the wrestler Trish Stratus, but I did not think Trish was a very good name for a dog. Tarja is the name for the beautiful and highly talented female vocalist of Finnish rock band Nightwish, who are one of my favorite musical acts of all time.

Although Tarja is as appealing to the eyes as her namesake, having what is known as the "dead grass pattern" and striking hazel-colored eyes, I did not know if that would be enough to get us through the airport. Sure, she is cute, but would she be cute enough to not get kicked off the plane if she barked the whole time we boarded?

I had to carry her on in a special dog carrying-bag on two flights from Sacramento, California, to Phoenix, Arizona. Then we had to fly from Phoenix to Houston. On the first flight, she only whined a few times, but on the second one, she yapped constantly for the first 20 minutes or so. Airline regulations prohibit even opening the bag and checking on the dog, but I cheated a bit to keep the peace in the coach section. I took off my left shoe, cracked open the bag, and stuck my foot in the bag for the rest of the flight. As long as she had my scent in there with her, she was fine and everyone around me was happy. Occasionally, she would nibble on my toe to let me know she was all right.

At home, she turned out to be an intense and highly intelligent puppy. She was house broken in four days with little discipline, and I had her retrieving a puppy bumper from a little swimming pool in my backyard within a week.

A few weeks later, I took her to her first lesson with a trainer in Crockett, and was greatly pleased with the results. She retrieved a quail with no problem, and then a pigeon. When the trainer, Laura Gibson, broke out a mallard, Tarja was a bit nervous. After all, this duck was her size. We did not force her to retrieve, and tried again in an hour. This time, she went up to it, barked a few times, and then grabbed it by its beak and carried it back to us. I was one seriously proud papa.

There is something special about watching an animal do what it was created to do. These dogs, just like Labs and goldens, were bred to retrieve ducks and love water, and so far, Tarja does a good job at both. We will have to wait and see how she does long-term in her training. Right now, there are a few hurdles to overcome such as biting our pant legs. My wife Lisa and I cannot walk out into the yard without Tarja grabbing our pants leg and wanting to play. When you tell her "No!" she does not quit. Well, at least the first five or six times we say it.

Then there is her propensity to want to chase everything she comes across. When I bring her to my parent's house, she chases their full-grown Australian shepherd around as if she were the puppy and Tarja the adult. She does not stop until we separate them; it is a bit annoying.

I realize she is only 10 weeks old as of this writing and is already showing good hunting instincts, combined with the breed's deserved reputation for hard-headedness. In other words, she is doing what she is supposed to be doing. I can't wait until she is fully trained and ready to go hunting.

I have a seven-year-old chocolate Lab at home named Sable. She was never trained to hunt and is simply a family pet—a wonderful one, I might add. Sable is one of the sweetest dogs I have ever been around, and I know she is closer to the end of her life than she is the beginning, and every time I see her and her "sister," Chyna, a German shepherd of the same age, I can't help but think my years with them are limited. That makes me sad, as those two dogs—which have been babied to the fullest—are members of the family, and have been loyal, loving companions. Then I think about Tarja, my new pup, and know there is new blood in the household, one that will be a hunting partner for years to come. That brings a big smile to my face, even though sometimes that smile is hard to muster because I am so tired from keeping up with her.

RETRIEVER PROFILES

In Texas, Labradors are by far the most common retriever, with black, chocolate, and yellow varieties fairly evenly divided among the population. There are other retrievers used in the Lone Star State, too, and it is worth a look at the profile of a few of them before deciding which would better suit your needs.

LABRADOR RETRIEVER

It is hard to beat a Lab. These dogs are hard working, eager to please their owners, and are probably the sweetest natured of all of the big dog breeds. According to the American Kennel Club (AKC): "The ideal disposition is one of a kindly, outgoing, tractable nature; eager to please and non-aggressive towards man or ani-

Black Labs are the standard issue, although chocolate and yellows have become increasingly popular in recent years.

A good Lab will be as interested in watching the ducks come in as is the hunter.

mal. The Labrador has much that appeals to people; his gentle ways, intelligence, and adaptability make him an ideal dog. Aggressiveness towards humans or other animals, or any evidence of shyness in an adult, should be severely penalized."

I have seen a few mean Labs in my time, and a number of them that were protective of their owner's vehicles, but most of the time, they are sweethearts and have more fun than even the hunters out in the field.

My father's late friend had a Lab that was so eager to

Yellow Labs make beautiful photo subjects.

get into the water, he had to tie it in the boat while riding down the river. That is not exactly desirable behavior, but you have to respect the enthusiasm.

Labs are great dogs for most hunting applications you find in Texas, from dry ground goose hunts to hunting ducks in the coastal marsh. Their overall willingness to please makes them a great first choice for a hunting dog.

GOLDEN RETRIEVER

If there is any dog that competes with the Lab in the friendliness department, it is the golden retriever. These dogs are more popular as family dogs than working hunters in Texas, but they do have their following.

The AKC notes that a golden is very graceful when trotting: "Gait is free, smooth, powerful, and well coordinated, showing good reach. Viewed from any position, legs turn neither in nor out, nor do feet cross or interfere with each other. As speed increases, feet tend to converge toward centerline of balance. It is recommended that dogs be shown on a loose lead to reflect true gait. Golden retrievers are friendly, reliable, and trustworthy. Quarrelsomeness or hostility towards other dogs or people in normal situations, or an unwarranted show of timidity or nervousness, is not in keeping with golden retriever character."

CHESAPEAKE BAY RETRIEVER

Chesapeakes have only a cult following in Texas. They were bred to hunt in the most hostile conditions of the North, but they are excellent retrievers with an intensity that cannot be matched. These dogs will stop at nothing to get what they are after, and that is what makes them excellent retrievers—and a bit hard to work with for beginning dog handlers and hunters. Yes, they are hardheaded.

Chesapeake Bay retrievers come in three primary colors: brown, sedge, and dead grass. The author's dog, pictured here, is dead grass, and at the time of this writing was only 11 weeks old and already showing signs of being a very intense and skilled retriever.

Chesapeakes are excellent swimmers and can handle many retrievers in deep and even current-laden waters. They are great dogs for those hunting big, open water, as their swimming skills are unmatched. Chesapeakes are popular as water rescue dogs and have saved more lives from drowning in the United States than any other species.

These are not the overly-friendly dogs that Labs or goldens are. In fact, some can be aloof around strangers and other dogs. Their reputation as being overly aggressive is not necessarily true. They are just not that impressed with people outside their family.

According to the AKC: "The Chesapeake Bay retriever should show a bright and happy disposition with an intelligent expression. Courage, willingness to work, alertness, nose, intelligence, love of water, general quality, and, most of all, disposition should be given primary consideration in the selection and breeding of the Chesapeake Bay retriever."

If you are looking for a dog that can take any kind of condition and has no fear, a Chesapeake might be for you. However, if you are a beginning hunter and want an easy-to-train, gregarious animal that can double as a lapdog, look elsewhere.

OTHER BREEDS

There are other retrieving breeds used in Texas, but only in small numbers. There is the Newfoundland, which is the species the Chesapeake

There is nothing like watching a retriever at work. The intensity in their eyes coupled their eagerness to please their owners is a remarkable sight.

derived from originally. These are big, intense dogs, preferred for hunting in cold climates. There are also a few curly-coated and smooth-coated retrievers around, as well as weimaraners trained for retrieving.

The coolest retriever I have ever seen was a big Doberman that was as adept as any other species at bringing in ducks

Chapter
Nineteen

Ducks in Trouble

All is not well in the world of waterfowl. While the populations of most species are in good shape, a few have very questionable futures. This includes one of Texas' most popular, sought-after, and symbolic ducks, the pintail.

Back in the 1970s, when the point system was in place, hunters could kill 10 pintails daily.

"On our club, which I used to share with outdoor writers Ray Sasser and Buddy Gough near High Island, we used to shoot pintails every day and almost always get our limit," said veteran waterfowler Lou Stagg of Broaddus. "We would only shoot drakes. There were enough pintails around that you could be that choosy."

In stark contrast, during the 2005-2006 season, hunters could take only one pintail a day, and that was only from December 22 until season's end. This "season within a season" was a response to a decline in pintail numbers that has seen bag limits for the beautiful bird drop steadily over the years to this low point.

U.S. Fish and Wildlife Service (USFWS) officials estimated the spring 2005 breeding population at 2.56 million birds.

Pintail populations are steady enough to allow hunting, but are a fraction of what they used to be.

That was up 17 percent from 2004 due to wetter conditions on the breeding grounds, but it was still 54 percent below the North American Waterfowl Management Plans (NAWMPA) goals for the species. NAWM-PA is an agreement between the United States and Canada (and later Mexico) signed in 1986 that seeks to get duck populations back to where they were during the 1970s. It is a goal that includes habitat conservation and restoration, but one that often leaves waterfowl managers and hunters frustrated, particularly with regard to pintail.

Much of this confusion centers on the fact that while other dabbling duck species bounced back after the prairie droughts of the 1980s, pintail numbers stayed in turmoil. In fact, by the early 1990s, pintail populations had dropped to less than a quarter of the 9 million-plus peak record hit in 1955.

USFWS statistics show that by 2002, pintail numbers hit a record low of 1.8 million birds. There has been some rebound due to better nesting conditions, but pintails populations are still at a fraction of where they used to be.

Pintails are susceptible to late winter freezes because they are the first duck to head north.

As with anything waterfowl-related issue, there is a litany of factors involved, but changes in habitat seem to be the major culprit. Pintails are unique ducks, not only in their long-necked, streamlined appearance, but also in behavior. They are the first ducks to leave wintering grounds and to nest in the spring, and this exposes them to deadly late season freezes.

While gadwall and teal, which both have seen major population increases, prefer tall-grass prairie for nesting, pintails use short-grass plains, farm fields, and shallow wetlands that expose them to numerous risks.

"Pintails play with a bad hand of cards all year long, especially given the way humans have changed the landscape," said Ducks Unlimited (DU) Canada waterfowl biologist Karla Guyn in an article in *National Wildlife.*

A prime example is in the Canadian prairie, the pintails preferred nesting grounds. Since the early 1980s, millions of acres of this region have changed from fall seeding to spring seeding. This has been severely detrimental to pintails, as studies by DU Canada have shown that fall seeded areas produce one successful pintail nest per 80 acres, while spring seeded areas produce one per 1000 acres.

Another change in Canadian agriculture has also hurt pintails. Farmers used to practice "summer fallowing" where they give cropland a rest every second summer. According to DU Canada, since the 1970s, farmers have converted 13 million acres of summer fallow to annual cropping in prime pintail breeding grounds.

"This massive land-use change sees more nesting in habitats that will likely be destroyed by farm machinery," said DU Canada's Pintail Initiative Project report. "Pintails will not re-nest as persistently as some other ducks. Therefore, pintails are less well adapted to deal with nest loss than other species."

The Pintail Initiative involves identifying key nesting areas and working with farmers to change some agricultural practices: "Research has identified that conversion of cropland to perennial forages (grass) can improve pintail nesting success. For two years, researchers searched over 2000 acres of hay land for duck nests. They found that pintails, on average, hatched one nest every 142 acres, nearly 10 times the number typically observed in spring-seeded cropland. Nearly 4000 acres of both fall-seeded crops, like winter wheat, and spring-seeded fields were searched over a two-year study. Pintails, on average, hatched one nest in every 72 acres of fall-seeded crops (in contrast to one nest in every 1,332 acres of traditional spring-seeded cropland).

"Fall-seeded crops generated a greater number of nests and from these nests, there was greater success in hatching ducks. Fall-seeded cereal crops are a pintail-friendly cropping alternative in areas where cropland intensification has encroached on traditional pintail breeding areas. They also benefit landowners. Winter wheat requires less chemical inputs and offers greater production, which can translate into greater revenues for producers."

There is another problem in pintail paradise: predators. The area's natural order involved the presence of antelope, bison, and the apex predator of the region, gray wolves. There were very few small mammalian predators and scavengers, as wolves do not tolerate their presence in the open prairie. As the bison was wiped out and antelope populations knocked down to remnant numbers, wolves were pushed aside and what packs survived were trapped, poisoned, and shot so they would not prey on livestock introduced to the area. This allowed the red fox, which was formerly not very common on the prairie, to flourish along with coyotes, minks, and badgers. These species are all major duck nest predators that have had a major effect on duck populations.

Then there is a less sinister looking but perhaps more effective nest predator, the raccoon. The natural prairie habitat is not very conducive to raccoons, but as man made changes to the region, it allowed 'coons to flourish. By the 1970s, 'coons took a strong hold on the region and are now very common to the point of being a major problem. Nesting success in some areas is as low as 0 to 7 percent, and 'coons do much of this damage.

The fragmentation of grasslands makes it easier for predators like 'coons to encounter duck nests and this puts pintails, in particular, in harms way.

Delta Waterfowl (Delta) conducted a study in the spring of 2000 in what they call the "moonscape" of southern Saskatchewan. This area has very little cover now and is perhaps the pintails greatest area of vulnerability.

In this study, Vance Lester of the University of Saskatchewan and Aaron Pearse of Idaho State kicked off a predator removal project on 16 square mile blocks near the town of Ceylon. Lester covered nest success while Pearse measured duckling survival. The control block (untrapped) had an 11 percent nest success while the trapped area had 28 percent. Duckling survival in the control area was 28 percent and 50 percent in the trapped area.

That was after only one year and predator control tends to become more effective after people have trapped it for a few seasons, showing that nest and duckling predation is a major problem for pintails.

SCAUP

Pintails however, are not the only duck species in peril. Scaup, known to most hunters as "bluebills," have declined greatly, forcing Central Flyway waterfowl managers to cut the bag limit from three to two, even though they are not a popular species in much of the region.

"Scaup are big-water birds, and for those of us who hunt the reservoirs, they are a staple of our harvest. When they cut us down to two birds, it was not worth it to us pursue them. What is troubling is there doesn't seem to be a true consensus on what's happening with them," said Sam Rayburn duck guide Roger Bacon.

The 2005 breeding scaup estimate was 3.39 million birds and that is down 46 percent from NAWMPA goals.

If the problems with pintails have scientists scratching their heads, the scaup situation could have them losing their hair.

"No one is quite sure exactly what the problem is with scaup. We know there are several factors at play, but no one has found that magic bullet yet," said DU biologist Jim Ringleman.

Ringleman said many scientists are looking at problems in the scaup's nesting habitat, the boreal forests of Canada, for clues: "Just like in the prairie breeding grounds, there are changes afoot in that forest region, and the scaup population decline is coinciding with it, although no one believes that alone is the problem."

Timber harvest and mining activities have increased greatly in that part of Canada over the last couple of decades Government officials in Ontario are considering allowing clear cuts as large as 25,000 acres, with nearly half the forest in the region slated for harvest in the next decade. Many in the waterfowl community are concerned that all of this activity could be having a negative effect on the scaup's breeding cycle, and that increased erosion caused by deforestation might be causing water quality problems in rearing ponds.

Others are more concerned about mining activities in the region and their effect on water quality. The water in the boreal forest region is high in nutrients, particularly, potassium, which bodes well for the invertebrates and

PHOTO COURTESY OF THE U.S. FISH AND WILDLIFE SERVICE

Problems with scaup populations are even more mysterious than the plight of the pintail.

tiny crustaceans that scaup eat. Most of these nutrients occur in the ground-water and some are scared that disturbances caused by mining could be halting these flows and having a negative effect on the scaup's preferred food.

"One thing that has been observed is the decline in freshwater shrimp populations in the scaup's range. Freshwater shrimp are a favorite food of scaup, and it makes sense that if a food supply of a species dwindles, so does

PHOTO COURTESY OF THE U.S. FISH AND WILDLIFE SERVICE

A declining population of freshwater shrimp in the prairie pothole region could be at the root of the scaup decline, according to some scientists.

the species in question," said Ringleman.

Another problem could be the zebra mussel, a mollusk from Asia accidentally introduced into North American waters a few decades ago. They have since covered the bottom of many northern reservoirs and rivers, and have staked a heavy claim in the Great Lakes region. They are filter feeders that have made formerly murky waters as clear as tap water. In fact, some areas in the Great Lakes have water visibility comparable to that of the Caribbean now. Scaup love to feed on zebra mussels and, unfortunately, zebra mussels contain dangerous levels of selenium, which can have negative effects on scaup physiology.

According to Delta, Dr. Scott Petrie's team at the Long Point Waterfowl Research Foundation has found elevated levels of selenium in both lesser and greater scaup during the winter and spring migration on Lake Ontario: "Scaup are accumulating selenium by feeding on abundant zebra mussels. Although elevated levels of selenium can cause stress or death in waterfowl, it is unknown whether scaup visiting the Great Lakes are able to eliminate the element prior to arrival on the breeding grounds."

Delta's research has also brought to light problems similar to those facing scaup in relation to predation. They note that scaup are a philopatic species, meaning that hens and their female offspring go back to the same area they were born to nest each year, and this makes them highly susceptible to "new" predators such as raccoons and red foxes.

In Bob Bailey's article, "An Achilles Heel for Bluebills," he wrote that eradication of nesting birds by newly introduced predators is a well-documented, worldwide phenomenon "caused by the impacts of human settlement, cultivation, and trade on the environment.

"Arctic foxes released on the Aleutian Islands nearly eliminated the Aleutian goose, a small relative of the Canada. A predator control program on the islands brought Aleutians back from the brink and it has now been removed from the list of U.S. endangered species. Other birds threatened by predators expanding on the heels of settlement, like shearwaters and oyster-catchers nesting on the beaches of East Coast islands in the U.S., have been saved by predator management."

He also wrote that the hen scaup's exceptional vulnerability to new predators on the prairies would make it one of the first ducks to disappear as the land was cultivated and settled: "As invading predators picked off hens, daughters, and nests on portions of the breeding range over time, there would be no survivors to home to the area. Unlike other species like blue-winged teal, scaup hens are highly philopatic, so there would be no reservoir of nomadic breeding females, shifting with changing patterns of water availability across the prairies each spring."

"For example, if all the hen teal were killed by predators (but even foxes would have trouble catching every teal) in any given spring on a section of breeding habitat, there could be twice as many teal appear on the area the following spring if the water conditions are favorable."

Raccoons, which were not in the plains region until a few decades ago, are responsible for destroying untold numbers of scaup and other duck nests.

PHOTO COURTESY OF THE U.S. FISH AND WILDLIFE SERVICE

Finally, some scientists believe that expectations for scaup numbers are simply too high. In a scaup specific workshop held in September 1999 in Jamestown, North Dakota, scientists debated this issue. One of the points brought up was scaup numbers have not met NAWMPA goals since 1984, and that waterfowl managers might want to consider creating new goals for lesser and greater scaup since federal officials count both species together in the surveys.

"We recommend that the NAWMPA population goal be a separate, measurable goal for each species and that the goal population size be determined by 2005," according to published reports.

That never happened.

CANVASBACKS

If the pintail is problematic and the scaup situation is strange, then canvasbacks represent a conservative comeback for a species that has never been incredibly abundant in recent history.

Canvasbacks have always been my favorite duck (the pintail is a close second), and for most of my life, they have been off-limits to harvest. During the 1970s and 80s, the federal government labeled them a "species of special concern" and there were even talks they might have to one day be listed as a "threatened species," a dubious distinction for species on the edge of endangerment like the bald eagle was at the time. By the mid 1990s, canvasback populations had soared above the NAWMPA goal of 540,000 breeding birds, and USFWS officials allowed hunters to harvest one bird. The comeback was in response to moist wetland areas, but according to some scientists, it is the species' lack of flexibility that has stopped them from really taking off. The birds have a very strict regimen and migration, and if an historical stopover lake is drained or the habitat is no longer suitable for them, they are extremely reluctant to change course and find new areas. This causes heavy stress on the birds, and when the hens return to breeding grounds they are stressed, causing some to die, others to have fewer eggs, and others not to nest at all.

Another problem is one that should be familiar by now: predation. Like with scaup and pintails, "new" predators like raccoons are hell on canvasback nests and hens, and are probably a limiting factor in the recovery of the species. For now, canvasback populations are okay, although with a species that has such specific requirements, it would not take much to cause a downward shift in the population. Ditto for scaup and pintail with their respective problems. Currently, waterfowl managers are keeping an eye on the numbers and working on ways to get them back at least to a semblance of what they used to be.

Blake Fischer of Winnie made a special trip to Sam Rayburn to get a canvasback drake for the wall, and was happy to see his dream realized.

It is worth mentioning that hunters should not feel guilty for taking any of these three species. Wildlife officials close-ly monitor harvest of these species and believe it has minimal impact on the popula-tions under the very conservative current provisions, if it has an impact at all.

Enjoy the gift of being able to hunt canvasback, pintail, and scaup and remind government officials and groups like DU and Delta that you want to see the popu-lations get back to goals set by NAWMPA, no matter what it takes. These ducks need our support so that our children's children will be able to hunt them 50 years from now.

Chapter Twenty

The Future of Waterfowling

What does the future hold for waterfowl hunting in Texas and beyond?

The answer depends on who you ask and what aspect of the waterfowl issue they understand best. There is no simple answer to what the future holds for those who crave the experience of hunting ducks and geese, and sharing a quiet morning on the water with a retriever. There are so many issues at hand that it boggles the mind to consider all of the factors that go into making a fall flight. For this final chapter, I have investigated these variables and broken them down into what I hope is an easily readable format that paints an accurate picture of the problems we are facing right now, and where they might take us in the not-too-distant future.

CHANGES IN THE LONE STAR STATE

As already stated, no single factor determines waterfowl hunting success or failure. Many dynamics can give hunters the blues or take them pleasantly by surprise. Take the first couple of weeks of the 2005-2006 seasons, for example.

Hunters during the previous four years had pitiful opening weekends and seasons. Most hunters were expecting the same for 2005-2006. During opening weekend, hunters at the J.D. Murphree Wildlife Management Area bagged more than three birds per hunter. Hunting was also much better than expected at the Anahuac National Wildlife Refuge, and in the marshes on the Louisiana side of the Sabine River as well. Joey Suire of Gist reported taking limits in the Burton's Ditch area, an area that faced tough conditions last season.

Why the good hunting despite extremely warm weather and a fair amount of marsh damaged by Hurricane Rita? The answers originate north and east of the region. Texas Parks & Wildlife Department officials reported the region around Dallas, east along the I-20 corridor, remains abnormally dry.

According to TPWD: "Hunters had fair to good shoots on Lake Fork, Toledo Bend, Caddo Lake, Lake O' the Pines, Lake Tawakoni, Cooper Lake, Ray Roberts, and Sam Rayburn. These lakes and reservoirs are holding the only available water, besides the rivers that feed them, and ducks are congregating on the limited moisture."

Over to the east, ducks found very little food in the marshes of southeastern Louisiana and Mississippi due to the incredible damage Hurricane Katrina did to wetlands there. The birds have to find food somewhere, and the closest spots are our marshes and fields and those in Southwest Louisiana not affected by Hurricane Rita's storm surge. The Holly Beach and Johnson Bayou areas are in bad shape, but some of the marshes around Hackberry and just south of Interstate 10 are in good shape.

Over the last few years, the areas listed above have been wet and in good condition, keeping ducks over there and offering overall more good food than they will find in Southeast Texas.

One of the biggest factors contributing to our lack of success in the last years has been rice production. Statewide production has dropped 62 percent over the last 30 years, but in Orange, Jefferson, Chambers, Liberty, Galveston, and Brazoria counties, it has dropped 73 percent, and much of that has been in the last 12 to 15 years. In 2002, the combined rice acreage of those counties was only 57, 336 acres.

Rice production near Wharton, Bay City, and Matagorda has also declined, but not as much as in the other areas, and the hunting has been much better down there over the last few years.

You will often hear duck and goose reports referred to as "east of Houston" and "west of Houston." That is because Houston is a real dividing line in terms of waterfowl habitat, and the area has had the worst end of the deal.

Another major factor in waterfowl success has been hunting pressure, and that is something hunters in Southeast Texas put on ducks in a big way. In 1990, there were 60,000 duck hunters in Texas, and by the year 2000, there were 120,000. This put great pressure on public lands in particular, and moved ducks toward areas with little pressure.

The High Plains region of Texas has less than 2 percent of the duck hunting pressure in the state, yet 2005's midwinter survey showed it holding 450,000 ducks. The Rolling Plains region just west of Dallas held 700,000 ducks, and the Oak/Blackland Prairie Region from Fort Worth east to the Pineywoods held some 600,000 birds.

For comparison, in the year 2000, the High Plains only held about 125,000 ducks and the Rolling Plains held around 400,000. That shows a huge buildup of ducks in a few years in that region, and a decline in Southeast Texas that corresponds perfectly.

"There is simply a lack of pressure in much of the state," said guide Roger Bacon. "I take a group up to the Panhandle every year now, and have learned no one hunts ducks up there. You cannot find steel shot west of Forth Worth, so if you go, bring your own shot because they're not going to have it.

"It just makes sense, where there is food, water, and the least pressure, there are going to be ducks."

PROBLEMS ON THE NESTING GROUNDS

For every 1 percent decline in native grasslands in the Prairie Pothole Region of the U.S. and Canada, there will be 25,000 fewer ducks in the fall. Consider that the current loss rate is 2.5 percent a year, and you can see there are big problems for ducks and duck hunters to face right now. That means there are 62,500 fewer ducks annually, and in 14 years, that number equals 875,000. This does not factor in the annual fluctuation due to drought, predation, and other factors. This is simply that acreage lost to farming and

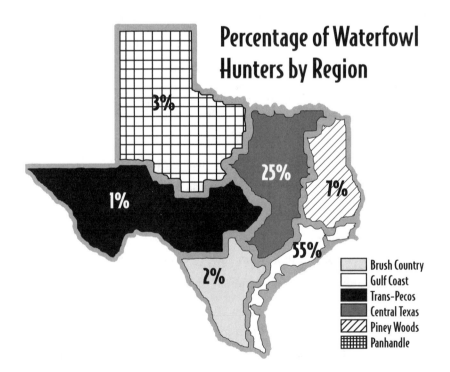

Percentage of Waterfowl Hunters by Region

3%
25%
1%
1%
55%
2%

Brush Country
Gulf Coast
Trans-Pecos
Central Texas
Piney Woods
Panhandle

development in that crucial region of North America translates to ducks nature can never produce.

Duck hunters on the Texas Coast faced very poor hunting during 2002-2004, and while there are numerous factors affecting the region during the fall migration, the fact is if current trends continue in the Prairie Pothole Region, things will only get worse.

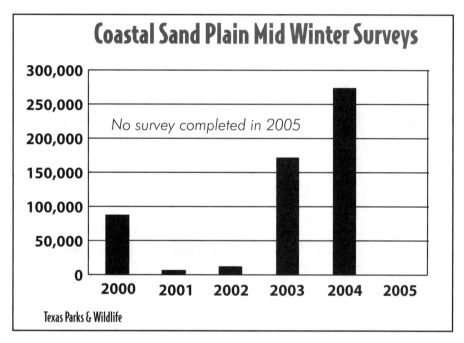

"That area really is the most crucial zone, and pretty much is the duck factory of the country. The issues that affect ducks there end up affecting hunters in Texas," said Jim Ringelman, Director of Conservation Programs for Ducks Unlimited (DU).

That region of the country has typically been ranching country, and according to Ringelman, cattle and ducks work well together: "Cattle and ducks have much of the same needs. They need grass and they need water. The problem comes when people convert ranches to farmland. The big farms like to drain the ponds because they can grow crops on the pond acreage, and that gives the ducks less habitat for nesting."

DU has been working on what they call "conservation easements," where they work out an agreement with landowners to pay them a fee for what the farmed area of wetlands on the property would be worth if converted to cropland. In exchange, the landowners must not develop the wetlands.

"Easements are a great way for us to keep some of these wetlands intact and try to preserve what we have," Ringelman said.

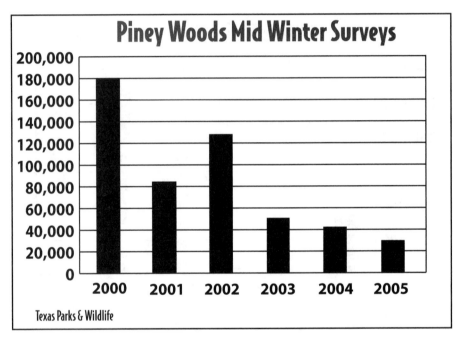

A different kind of problem comes in the form of nesting success related to predation. There are different kinds of predators in the region than were there even 50 years ago, such as raccoons, which were typically not present on the plains historically. Red foxes and skunks are also in much higher numbers than ever due to the bottom falling out of the trapping market, and government trappers becoming an endangered species.

For illustration, say 100 hens lay 500 female eggs, and on the second try lay 353 female eggs for a total of 853 female eggs; 50 percent of those nests will be destroyed on the first nesting, and some 35 percent will perish on the second nesting. You can assume 128 female ducklings survive to hatch.

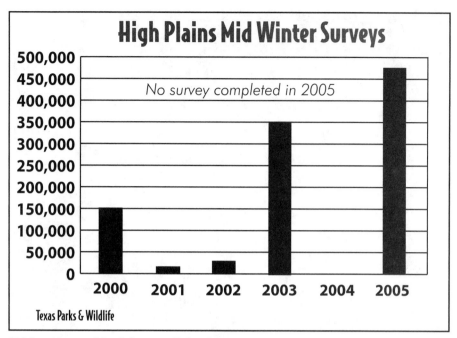

High Plains Mid Winter Surveys

No survey completed in 2005

Texas Parks & Wildlife

DU estimates 82 of those will die during brood rearing, and 42 hens will survive to fly south.

Predators are not only major problems in the prairie region, but also in Texas and other areas where species like wood and mottled duck nest.

A study on wood duck and hooded merganser nesting success conducted by the University of Georgia showed that rat snakes alone destroyed 4 percent of all wood duck nests in the study area—sometimes killing the hens. According to the study: "The death of an incubating hen has a greater potential impact on the population than the loss of a clutch or the loss of individual hatchlings, because that hen can make no further contribution to the population. Black rat snake [close cousin to our Texas rat snake] predation on incubating wood duck and hooded merganser hens and nests could have a significant impact on the reproductive success of populations using natural cavities in southeastern river swamp ecosystems."

A later study conducted by the University of Georgia showed that the black rat snake "readily circumvented predator shields and was the only

PHOTO COURTESY OF THE U.S. FISH AND WILDLIFE SERVICE

Research on the nesting grounds shows that predators put a big dent in the potential winter flight.

known nest predator during the five years of observation. This species destroyed 24 of 76 nests (32 percent) initiated from 1973-1975."

A Texas study showed that fire ants destroyed, "three of 20 clutches in wood duck nest boxes."

A University of Michigan study revealed: "Within the first two weeks of hatching, 86 to 90 percent of the chicks die. A main cause of mortality is predation." The study listed owls, minks, raccoons, foxes, and rat snakes as chief predators of baby wood duck.

On the Texas coast, mottled duck numbers have been in decline over the years, and much of that can likely be attributed to predation. In a study entitled, *The American Alligator as a Predator of mottled ducks*, researchers Ruth M. Elsey, Phillip L. Trosclair III, and Jeb T. Linscombe found that alligators might do more damage to mottled duck populations than some researchers formerly believed. According to the report: "Although the alligator has been noted to prey upon mottled duck, evidence of mottled duck consumption is rare in numerous studies of alligator food habits. This may be due to the season and habitat from which alligators were collected for evaluation (often autumn samples from deep water habitats preferred by adult alligators). We examined stomach contents of alligators in summer (when mottled duck broods and molting adults are flightless) from shallow water habitats preferred by mottled ducks. Mottled duck remains were found in 20.9 percent of 43 alligator stomachs examined, far more than the highest frequency occurrence previously reported (1.27 percent). Unexpectedly, three relatively small alligators (1.51-1.70 meters total length) consumed mottled ducks and the sixteen largest alligators did not. This study underscores the importance of season and location of collections when evaluating stomach content data."

Retired Texas Parks & Wildlife Department biologist Charles Stutzenbaker literally wrote the book on mottled duck in 1988 with, *The Mottled Duck, its Life History and Management*. In that book, he wrote: "...the alligator is the single most efficient predator of adult mottled ducks and ducklings."

THE DUCK COMMANDER SPEAKS

Phil Robertson is serious about ducks and duck hunting. Known to waterfowlers around the nation as "the Duck Commander," the West Worgan, Louisiana, resident is renowned for his superior hunting skills, entertaining home videos, and no-nonsense attitude. I had the great pleasure of sharing a couple of days with Robertson at his home/headquarters and in a duck blind in a beautiful flooded bottom in North-Central Louisiana during the last week of the 2005-2006 season. I have always respected his perspective on waterfowl hunting and conservation, and during our meeting, it did not take long to find out he believes serious changes are needed for there to be a future for duck hunting.

"The greatest detriment to duck hunting is what is called 'the federal refuge system'," Robertson said. "It sounds great that the ducks will have a place to rest and all, but in reality it makes hunting very difficult, as it does not take them long to figure out where they are being shot and where there is no pressure."

By law, hunting and fishing are considered "priority" uses of refuge land, but that leaves vast tracts of the 110 million of acres of refuges off limits to hunting. Robertson, who hunts all around the country, said when scouting locations to film hunts for his home videos, he goes as far away from refuges as possible: "You can literally watch the ducks pile into the no-hunting areas. A lot of guys will get excited because they get a duck hole near a refuge, but soon learn that it works against them in most cases."

A big part of the problem according to Robertson is that most of the refuges are in the flyways and wintering areas, not in the prairie pothole or "duck factory" region where they nest. This is a fact the U.S. Fish and Wildlife Service boasts of on their website: "Most of the more than 520 National Wildlife Refuges and additional Waterfowl Production Areas managed by the Fish and Wildlife Service are located along the migratory flyways, serving as breeding and wintering grounds and as 'rest stops' for these birds. For example, in the 'duck factory' of the upper Midwest, the National Wildlife Refuge System manages just 2 percent of the landscape, yet 23 percent of the region's waterfowl breed there."

"It doesn't make sense to have all of this refuge land in areas where the ducks winter if you're trying to do something about duck production," Robertson said. "They keep telling us we are losing crucial breeding grounds, but they keep buying refuge land down in the wintering areas."

Just as frustrating for him as the presence of so much refuge land off-limits to hunting is the lack of predator control programs in the Prairie Pothole Region: "Pretty much everyone agrees we are losing about 85 percent of our ducks before they ever fly down due to predation in the nesting areas. Think about that for a second. What we get to fly down is around 15 percent of the potential ducks. If you have a total flight of 100 million ducks, decreasing predation by only 5 percent would add 30 million ducks to that. If you could ever get predation down to around 70 percent, you could pretty much double the fall flight every year."

Robertson said he believes if hunters knew just how much of a role raccoons, foxes, mink, and

Phil Robertson, "the Duck Commander," is a lifelong, dedicated waterfowler with a fascinating perspective on the future of the sport.

other predators played in duck production dynamics, they might support paying more for federal duck stamps to support predator control: "No one wants to wipe out the predators. God put them here to do their role, but he also put ducks here for us to hunt and to eat, and we can balance things out if we put the effort into it. With fur being out of fashion because of the animal rights people, and very little trapping, you have a situation where you have more predators on the breeding grounds than ever, and we are seeing the results every fall."

Robertson believes that ducks should not be managed by the U.S.

Fish and Wildlife Service, but by the Department of Agriculture: "They should view them as a food source and a cash crop like cattle, sheep, or corn. If you get a boll weevil outbreak, they do whatever it takes to eliminate that problem. If we took that stance with ducks and their predators, we would likely have the skies black with them again like we did many years ago."

Another problem Robertson sees is overbearing federal regulations and a lack of understanding of ducks and duck hunting by federal game wardens: "We were hunting in South Texas and had a federal warden tell us we were over our limit on redheads [two birds]. The warden thought the green-winged teal [limit six] were redheads. The warden was ready to give us a ticket."

There are virtually no similarities between redhead and green-winged teal. Teal are tiny ducks, redhead are big ducks. Redhead, as the name implies, have a red head, and greenwings have a reddish orange head, and the drakes have a green stripe down the middle. There are other differences as well.

Robertson eventually won the argument over the ducks' identification, but said it showed there is a lack of training in federal game wardens: "They get 13 weeks of training, and very little of it on duck identification. I think the wardens should be required to have a hunting license and duck stamp if they are going to have the power of the federal government that they can bring down on you. They should be required to hunt 10 days out of a season."

Robertson said he has nothing against wardens, but duck hunting regulations are complex, and wardens should have an intimate understanding of the laws before they enforce them: "This is what I do; I am a duck hunter, and I hunt every day of the season. I want to make sure that people will be able to have quality duck hunting 100 years from now, and unless we change some things, that is just not going to happen. Hunting can be good at times now, but we can make it a whole lot better."

GLOBAL WARMING

"Left unchecked, global warming and associated climate change could affect North America's waterfowl and habitat in a number of ways." — *A Waterfowler's Guide to Global Warming, National Wildlife Federation*

To be honest, I have never given much thought to global warming. I have always believed that any warming we are experiencing is most likely due to natural climatic changes and probably has little to do with pollution. When I read that quote from the National Wildlife Federation (NWF) study, I started rethinking things a bit.

According to the study: "Ducks, geese and other migratory waterfowl face substantial population declines during this century in North America from a warmer climate and shrinking wetlands habitat caused by global warming."

"Ducks and geese that use America's flyways face a trifecta of troubles caused by global warming, including major loss of prime breeding grounds, a reduction of coastal winter habitat, and disruptions in migration," said NWF President Larry Schweiger.

According to NWF, already in northern breeding habitats, where they say global warming has already gained a strong foothold, ducks and geese are responding by breeding earlier and expanding their ranges farther north.

"Global warming is setting up ducks and geese for a Pandora's box of problems that could devastate populations across the nation," Schweiger said. "We must not allow global warming to take our nation's waterfowl legacy away from our children. Global warming poses a basic threat to our conservation tradition. It challenges our responsibility to be good stewards of the water, land, and wildlife. I am confident that sportsmen will lead the way in overcoming this challenge."

"We are looking at a possible trifecta of pressures all convening within a few decades," said Patty Glick, global warming specialist for the NWF and the report's author.

The report, "looks at how projected global warming could affect waterfowl in each of the four North American flyways: Atlantic, Mississippi, Central, and Pacific. One of the most startling findings is in research by top waterfowl experts in North America suggesting that global warming could reduce wetland habitat in the Prairie Pothole Region by up to 91 percent by 2080. This could result in a decline in duck breeding pairs of anywhere from 9 to 69 percent, the research shows. Species at particular risk include mallard, gadwall, blue-winged teal, northern pintail, canvasback, redhead and ruddy duck."

According to Glick: "As the climate warms and evaporation and plant transpiration increase, many of these ponds are likely to dry up or be wet for shorter periods, making them less suitable habitat for breeding pairs and duck broods."

"Waterfowl are part of an American wildlife tradition that we cannot afford to lose," said George Meyer, executive director of the Wisconsin Wildlife Federation, a co-sponsor of the report. "The millions of ducks, geese and cranes Americans love depend on the health of the Prairie Potholes as a breeding ground, and we could be leaving ducks high and dry by the end of the century."

NWF officials also said: "Waterfowl also are facing the loss of up to 45 percent of the coastal wetlands they depend on in winter due to a possible 3- to 34-inch rise in average sea level by 2100. Especially vulnerable are the shallow wetlands of the Gulf and Atlantic coasts. These regions provide important wintering habitat for diving ducks such as canvasback, redhead, ruddy duck, and scaup.

"Warmer fall and winter temperatures in northern regions may reduce seasonal ice cover, making it unnecessary for ducks and geese to fly as far south to find ice-free water and adequate food.

"Thawing permafrost and changes in the vegetation of boreal forests and tundra regions of Alaska and Canada also could affect important breeding habitat for a number of North America's waterfowl species.

"Even where changes associated with global warming alone might not cause problems, the combined effects from human activities such as oil and gas development, forestry, mining, and global warming make it difficult for some waterfowl to adapt to a rapidly changing environment. Waterfowl face an uphill battle."

The NWF report stated that climate scientists point to carbon pollution as the primary culprit behind global warming: "In the last 100 years, global temperature rose by an average of 1 degree Fahrenheit, but in places such as Alaska, the change has been more dramatic. The average temperature in Alaska has risen by 5-7 degrees Fahrenheit in the last century, and is beginning to cause problems associated with softening permafrost and erosion along the state's coastline. Temperatures globally are projected to rise on average by between 2 to 10 degrees Fahrenheit in the coming decades, primarily because of carbon pollution from burning fossil fuels that is trapping heat from being released in the atmosphere. A 1 degree Fahrenheit rate of change in temperature in 100 years is faster than any time in recorded history."

This is an issue that certainly deserves more looking into, and I recommend anyone interested in the subject go to www.nwf.org and download the report. Just type "waterfowl" into their search engine and the .pdf file of the report will be one of the first documents that show up.

Again, I am skeptical of some of the global warming politics that has been kicked around over the years, but the data in this report is hard to deny.

ANIMAL RIGHTS

Waterfowl hunting is the next major target of the animal rights movement. The Humane Society of the United States (HSUS) is always the group I look at to see what play the movement is going to make. Sure, People for the Ethical Treatment of Animals (PETA) publicly release extreme, asinine, and downright lame comments, but HSUS has credibility with the mainstream media and the American public, who think of them as the saviors of abandoned puppies and kittens. Pretty much everyone knows PETA members are kooks.

HSUS, however, is the most well-funded, slick, and dangerous animal rights group, out to eradicate hunting. If you have doubts, then check out these excerpts from a HSUS press release:

> In a report, titled *The Ones That Almost Got Away: Unseen Victims of Waterfowl Hunters*, the HSUS documents the inaccuracies of previous research on waterfowl mortality and calls for efforts from wildlife management communities to dramatically reduce waterfowl wounding rates. Among the report's findings: "Wounding is an inherent component of waterfowl hunting. The majority of ducks and geese wounded in this way are not likely to recover; for these birds, death can be protracted. It is not currently possible to accurately document waterfowl wounding rates or to assess the total number lost to wounding. However, visible evidence for crippling, a more easily observed form of wounding, is more readily obtainable. Crippling rates of up to 45 percent of all birds shot have been documented via direct observation of hunts in progress.
>
> "Sampling procedures in earlier studies on the frequency of wounding and crippling were fundamentally flawed, as they generally relied on hunters' self reports, via questionnaires or surveys, to estimate wounding rates. The reliability of such figures is doubtful, since hunters may simply not accurately recall events of the hunt, may intentionally lie because they failed to retrieve shot birds, or may not see the wounding

or crippling they cause.

"One study comparing direct observation of waterfowl hunting with hunters' reports found a significant discrepancy between the numbers of birds wounded reported by the hunters and the tallies of trained, concealed observers. Hunters' self-reporting produced a crippling rate of 6 to 18 percent of all ducks and geese shot, while observers reported a crippling rate between 20 to 40 percent.

"A sophisticated mathematical reanalysis of U.S. crippling data estimates that for every duck killed, another is crippled. Skilled hunters wound approximately five ducks for every 10 killed outright, and novice hunters wound between five and 15 ducks for every 10 killed.

"In order to quickly kill a duck or goose, a shot must be fired within the appropriate range for the type of pellet being used. When a hunter shoots at a bird outside of the lethal range of the pellet, a practice known as "skybusting," the animal is often wounded or crippled but not killed outright. Aim error is also a factor in waterfowl wounding.

"Misidentification of protected species of ducks and geese are also at risk of similar wounding or crippling rates."

The report highlights hunters' inability to correctly identify under hunting conditions more than two or three of the most common duck species. Despite this, hunters shoot at more than 90 percent of ducks and 100 percent of geese they believe are within range.

While hunter education programs may produce some success in reducing waterfowl wounding and crippling rates, the report notes that hunter density and social factors may counteract educational efforts. The report posits that hunters may feel in competition with each other, driving them to be indiscriminate in their shooting in an attempt to kill more birds. Similarly, observing other hunters engaging in skybusting may result in acceptance of this practice. These social factors may increase as hunter density increases, as on firing lines, for example.

"Despite the realization that millions of ducks and geese are shot and injured, and suffer terribly before they die, there has been no comprehensive response from the wildlife management community to try to reduce the wounding rates," said the report's author, Robert Alison, Ph.D., Canadian waterfowl biologist, international waterfowl expert, and former waterfowl hunter who has written for outdoor and hunter magazines. In fact, states have programs in place designed to attract children to duck hunting. This will undoubtedly increase the percentage of waterfowl experiencing a prolonged, miserable death."

This is typical animal rights propaganda. They mix a little truth (wounding rates) with a lot of hyperbole. They forget to mention that waterfowlers pay to produce these ducks through duck stamp sales, excise taxes, and membership in groups like DU and Delta.

Be forewarned, this is the next great animal rights battle, and waterfowlers should be prepared.

MY SOLUTIONS

After studying the issues surrounding waterfowl management, I have concluded that there are a number of key things we could be doing to not only keep duck numbers in good shape, but expand them along with hunting

opportunities in the future. The problems we are having now are the culmi-
nation of years of wrong thinking, and I say it is time to take drastic measures
to change that. My solutions include:

BUY MORE NESTING GROUNDS

After talking with the Duck Commander, I say it is time U.S. Fish
and Wildlife Service (USFWS) officials do something about this and redi-
rect their land acquisition policy toward the breeding grounds and away from
the wintering grounds. Much of the breeding occurs in a handful of counties,
yet USFWS manages only a fraction of that habitat.

On the other hand, USFWS is the single largest landowner in
Jefferson County with the McFadden and Texas Point National Wildlife
Refuges. Ditto for other counties along the coast. Yes, it is good that those
lands have protection from development, and yes, they do produce native mottled duck, but they are a prime example of something USFWS has been
doing wrong all along. It makes no sense to have literally millions of acres conserved in wintering grounds throughout the country when nesting and breeding grounds are in trouble. Keeping the Prairie Pothole region away from
going under the plow would be a much better investment than adding to the
Trinity National Wildlife Refuge, for example. That is a big chunk of hard-
wood bottoms they have purchased along the Trinity River, yet hunters are
extremely limited as to where they can hunt.

Wouldn't it make a lot more sense to spend the valuable duck stamp
funds generated by hunters on areas that produce ducks? Wouldn't that be
better serving constituents than continue buying up land in the wintering
grounds and allowing hunting only in an extremely limited fashion?
Conserving more wintering grounds for waterfowl while the areas that actually produce those waterfowl are disappearing at a rapid pace is an idea
whose time has passed. USFWS should stop buying land in the wintering

grounds and buy land that will keep the duck factory producing.

I am on record being against the government buying any more land (which is a whole other topic), but that doesn't seem like that will be happening any time soon. If they are going to continue land acquisition with money from duck stamp sales and other means, they should buy the land that produces the ducks we hunt.

Conservation means the "wise use of resources" and continually buying up wintering grounds when nesting areas are perishing is not wise in any way, shape, or form.

CONTINUALLY RENEW CRP

The conservation easements that DU is involved with are an excellent way to keep duck production habitat intact, but it is not enough. A popular program part of the federal Farm Bill, the Conservation Reserve Program (CRP) is essential to keeping duck populations at or near current levels.

CRP is essentially a subsidy program where the federal government pays landowners to keep land as wildlife habitat, and a big part of that is preserving native grasslands and wetlands in the Midwest. I am generally against government subsidies, but until we stop subsidizing studies to determine the effects of cattle farting on the ozone layer, and giving foreign aid to countries that hate us, the least we can do is support ducks with taxpayer funds.

DU estimates there have been 4.7 million acres added to the Dakotas alone under CRP, and that nesting success there is 46 percent higher than if it were cropland. DU also estimates CRP recruits about 2 million ducks into the population every year that would not be there otherwise.

"If we lose CRP, we lose a lot, so its important that when it comes back up for renewal in 2007 with the Farm Bill, that hunters write their congressmen and senators and ask for support on this highly important issue," said Rogers Hoyt, senior vice president for DU in the South Central Region. "We had a lot of hunters get into duck hunting in the 1990s after CRP was in place, and they experienced the big boom that it caused in populations. Now that other factors are causing problems, some of these hunters do not realize how the hunting was before CRP was there, and many have not heard much about the effects of the program because it mainly takes place in the breeding grounds. But that is where it counts."

PREDATOR CONTROL

When you lose as much as 86 percent of nests in some areas of the Prairie Pothole region, there is a serious, serious problem. Experts agree that the best "natural" nesting success is around 20 percent. That means four out of five ducklings die before making it to the fall flight.

It has come time to start whacking some predators.

Delta Waterfowl (Delta) is a major supporter of predator control, and their studies show nest production on trapped areas versus adjacent non-trapped areas being more than three times higher than the average.

According to a press release sent out by Delta in 2004:

> This spring, Delta had eight 36-square-mile predator blocks covering 184,320 acres scattered across the Prairie Pothole Region (PPR) of North Dakota. Each site had a professional trapper who removed nest predators like raccoons and skunks during the breeding season.
>
> Five of the eight sites were monitored for nest success, and two of those were paired with untrapped (control) sites that contained similar habitat and densities of breeding ducks.
>
> The Cando site in the drift prairie of northeastern

North Dakota reported a remarkable 86 percent nest success, the highest in the 10 years Delta has conducted large-scale trapping. Overall, the trapped blocks averaged 57 percent nest success.

Research has shown that ducks must achieve 15 to 20 percent nest success in order to maintain the existing population, but scientific research showed that across much of the PPR, nest success had slipped below that level by 1990.

Nest-raiding and hen-eating predators are known to be the major reason that nest success had slipped below maintenance levels. All the monitored sites were well above the break-even level.

The Minnewauken site reported 62 percent nest success, Pleasant Lake was 53 percent, Walsh had 43 percent, and Harlow 42 percent.

"Ducks that don't get out of the egg don't migrate," says Delta President Rob Olson. "And once again, our predator work dramatically increased nest success. We're proving that predator management works, and that it works on a large scale."

The control blocks also achieved high nest success, one coming in at 37 percent and the other at 27 percent.

"The U.S. Fish and Wildlife Service helps us pick the areas for our predator management work. Those areas typically comprise 20 to 40 percent grass nesting cover. Modeling work by USFWS suggests we should see nest success in the 15 to 20 percent break-even level on those sites," said biologist Joel Brice, who heads up the predator management program for Delta.

Because nest success varies over space and time, it

doesn't surprise us when we get a control site that achieves high nest success. We're always pleased when we see high nest success on the untrapped sites. After all, high nest success is what it takes to produce ducks.

We also need to look at killing more alligators along the Texas coast. We have already noted that TPWD officials estimate the population in Orange, Jefferson, and Chambers Counties alone is at 283,000. There is no estimate for the rest of the state, but it could be as high as 500,000. There is no wonder that mottled duck numbers are in bad shape, as alligators are their chief predators as adults.

TPWD has coddled alligators for too long, and it is time to allow increased harvest in a big way. They allow hunters to kill up to four deer a season in Orange, Jefferson, and Chambers counties, and the deer populations there are miniscule compared to 283,000 alligators. It makes no sense. Allowing increased harvest of alligators could make a big difference with the populations of mottled duck, and allow hunters to score on some tasty alligator meat.

Critics say you cannot control predators throughout all of the nesting grounds, and that is true. Delta's approach is to focus on the essential areas, and since much of the habitat work for ducks is annual anyway, predator control will be no different from other measures employed.

What is different is the politics of it. Some have said controlling predators will garner necessary criticism from the animal rights crowd that is already down on our beloved sport. Who cares? Not me, because these groups are out to stop what we are doing anyway. Bending to their criticism is only showing weakness and makes what we are doing seem like its wrong when it is perfectly natural. Let science lead the way, not the emotions of activist groups who do not have a clue to begin with.

Predator control has a place in waterfowl management, and with states like Louisiana subsidizing Delta's predator control program, we might see just how effective it is over the next decade

DUCK STOCKING

In Texas, we have done very successful stocking of eastern turkeys in the Pineywoods region, and ringneck pheasants in the Panhandle. If we can pull that off, why not stock ducks? If we could get quality wild broodstock of mallard, teal, gadwall, and other species, I do not see why we could not establish populations that breed here in Texas. Areas like the Panhandle and South Texas Brush Country have plenty of small ponds and lakes that would make great breeding grounds. Yes, we have plenty of predators, but no more than they have up in the Prairie Pothole Region.

Such an experiment might fail. The ducks might decide to follow their *compadres* up north during the return flight in the spring, but then again, it could establish something very positive for us here in Texas. It might create ducks that breed and winter here.

I say we allow access to breeding ducks and eggs approved by the state and federal wildlife officials for private landowners and hunting clubs interested in doing this, and see what happens. We certainly have nothing to lose.

SELL RICE TO CUBA

Earlier in this chapter, we discussed rice production in parts of Texas dropping 73 percent in the last 30 years. Rice production is a major drawing card for ducks, and a lack of it has certainly hurt us. This, unfortunately, is another area where politics come into play.

Texas officials are lobbying for increased trade with Cuba, which is interested in buying lots of long-grained rice. The Treasury Department recently began requiring Cuba to pay for any goods before they are shipped to the U.S., which hurt the little trade that went on between the two countries.

A clause in a spending bill put before Congress in September of 2004 would have revived the rice trade. From an article in the *Houston Chronicle*: "President Bush, whose administration is steadfastly opposed to expanding trade with the communist country and dictator Fidel Castro, had threatened to veto the measure if House and Senate negotiators let the clause remain."

In the same article, U.S. Rep. Ted Poe, R-Humble, said: "It doesn't punish the communists in Cuba; it punishes the rice farmers in Texas."

I could not agree more with Poe.

We trade with China, which is also a communist country, and in 2006, according to the U.S. Census Bureau, we imported $15 billion more than we exported to them. Add to that the fact we spend billions buying oil from countries that support terrorism, and the big stance against rice trade with Cuba looks ridiculous. How does it make sense that we have open trade with the Saudis who produced most of the animals that flew planes into the World Trade Center and Pentagon, but we can't **sell** products to a country a few miles off our coast?

What would selling rice to Cuba hurt? There is no question it will benefit Texas farmers, and in turn ducks and duck hunters. Getting rice production back on track in a big way would greatly benefit us by giving ducks a reason to stick around in the winter.

SUPPORT GROUPS THAT ARE DOING SOMETHING

As you can see, the future of waterfowl hunting in our region relies on conservation, and unfortunately in politics.

Let's take conservation first.

We cannot help it if the winters are warm and most of the ducks never make it down this far. However, when they do reach our region, we can provide them with good habitat. While nesting habitat is the most crucial piece of the puzzle, we cannot overlook wintering habitat.

Without good wintering habitat, which means the right combination of water and food, ducks have no reason to stick around. There are plenty of other places in the state that have what they need, and have a whole lot less hunting pressure as well. We are losing quite a bit of land to development, which in a capitalistic society like ours is inevitable. More people equal more development. However, the land we are able to conserve also needs to be in good condition.

Take the marshes along the Intracoastal Canal corridor, for example. Channelization has allowed saltwater intrusion into formerly brackish marsh, and that has been extremely negative for waterfowl habitat, particularly in regards to certain foods ducks eat. For many years, no one looked at this problem, but since the boom in duck hunting popularity, the right people seem to be paying attention.

The Lower Neches Wildlife Management Area (WMA) in Bridge City is a shining illustration of good management. The Old River Unit has seen the benefits of erosion control and saltwater barriers. Ten years ago, there was very little vegetation there, and now there is increasing duck food and signs that marsh is coming back to life.

These measures are a joint effort of TPWD and DU. Over the last few years, DU has taken a bad rap for seemingly not doing enough habitat conservation in our region (The Texas Chenier Plain), but the facts show a different picture. Some 26 percent of all of DU's acreage in the Texas Prairie Wetlands Program lies within this range, and 66 percent of all of its public land projects lie within Orange, Jefferson, and Chambers counties.

"DU's main effort is in the Prairie Pothole Region, but we also understand the importance of winter habitat to ducks and the duck hunter, and have numerous projects going on in Southeast Texas to enhance habitat. We've restored, enhanced or conserved 100,000 acres of public waterfowl habitat in Texas at a cost of $6.7 million," said DU Texas' David Schuessler.

Schuessler said some critics have accused DU of excessive project work between Texas and the breeding grounds "short stops" annual waterfowl migration: "While we have performed 52,000 acres of critical habitat work in Oklahoma, Kansas, and Nebraska, there is no possible way these relatively few acres could alter migration."

The best thing we hunters can do it is to support organizations that promote waterfowl conservation and volunteer to help. In some areas there is starting to be an attitude of "I support DU" versus "I support Delta." The fact is, modern waterfowl hunting might not be here if it were not for DU and their powerful lobby and conservation ethic. In addition, Delta, although a much smaller organization, has some good ideas that deserve support and study. Both are good organizations.

Waterfowl hunters certainly do not always see eye to eye, but we can agree that we want a bright future for hunting, and that means continually pushing for conservation and sticking to our guns when it comes to the tough issues we face.

FINAL THOUGHTS

Duck and goose hunting is good now, but it can get better. Do not let all of the data regarding problems with conservation scare you. Ducks are not going extinct, and for the near future, we will have enough ducks to have lengthy seasons here in Texas. However, ignoring the problems we have would be a pitiful waste of the resource.

I am a big believer in "American Exceptionalism"—the concept that we are driven in this country to go beyond acceptable and push for

things that are exceptional. This is certainly true with wildlife management. We do not settle for things being "okay." We want game numbers
to be high, and the hunting experience to be amazing. Right now, the
hunting is good, but I believe it can be a whole lot better. If we push for
conservation that defies the politically correct tenets that we are operating
under, the future could be very bright.

*Waterfowl hunting is good right now, but it can get better. We have problems that are
serious, but there is time to correct them if we act now.*

In the meantime, always embrace the opportunities you have to hunt
these magnificently created creatures, and realize that they are a gift to those
who care the most about them—the hunters.

See you in the field.

Acknowledgements

Writing a thanks and acknowledgements section for a book is always challenging for me. There are so many people out there that help in so many ways that it is difficult sometimes to list them all and give them the fanfare they deserve.

Here goes...

The first thanks goes to my wife, Lisa, for putting up with my extreme dedication to the outdoors, particularly waterfowl and coastal fishing. I made 30 duck and goose hunts last year, and about 60 fishing trips on top of a dozen or so deer hunts, a few dove hunts, a turkey hunt, and a varmint hunt or two—and that was actually a slow outdoors year for me! Lisa never complained once, and I could not be a luckier man.

My parents are supportive of everything that I do, and they are, indeed, my biggest fans. Thanks for always being there.

Thanks to Don Zaidle for being a focused editor who will let only the best come out of me as a writer. There are not many people in this business who care as much as he does about the craft and the craftsmen.

Thanks to Duane Hruzek, and Roy and Ardia Neves of *Texas Fish & Game* for believing in me all of these years, and for giving me a chance to write stories and books for them. It is truly a labor of love for me. Also, to Nicole McKibbin for just being a plain cool person and hooking me up with awesome products to test.

Thanks to Hallie and Jerome Metzger for being very good friends. Hallie and I are not sure, but we might have been separated at birth, as we think and act so much alike, which should be frightening to the rest of the civilized world.

Thanks to Eric Adams, my partner in crime, for the dedication on our hunting project and for showing me that Yankees do actually know what they are talking about sometimes when it comes to hunting and fishing.

Thanks to David Schuessler and everyone at Ducks Unlimited in Texas for all of the help with data and for their undying support of waterfowl conservation.

Thanks to Bobby Caskey and everyone at Shoal Grass Lodge in Aransas Pass for all of the hospitality. You guys have an awesome place and know how to make someone truly feel at home.

Thanks to Brian Fischer, Blake Fischer, Shane Chesson, Harlon Hatcher, and everyone at the Drake Plantation for some awesome hunts and for being the most open, giving people with which I have ever shared a blind.

Thanks to Will Beaty of Central Flyway Outfitters. Will not only runs a top-notch operation, but also is one of the best interviews regarding waterfowl in the business.

Thanks to Phil "Duck Commander" Robertson for inviting me out to hunt, and for the best pot of duck gumbo I have ever had. Your insight on the waterfowling experience is inspiring.

Thanks to Buck Gardner for his wonderful advice on duck hunting and for sharing one of the greatest times I have ever spent in a blind. Also for nicknaming me, "King of the Buffleheads." Gotta love it!

Thanks to Ted Nugent for his friendship over the last 14 years, and for always defending hunting and common sense values. There will never be another like him, although we could use about 1000 more to straighten out things.

Thanks to Capt. Skip James for being one of the funniest people I have ever met, and for always being there for me. True friends are hard to come by, and he is one of the good guys in my book.

Thanks to Ronnie Friend for keeping things going in my musical endeavors, and to my bandmates in FREAK13 and Drachen for giving me a place to express the music I hear in my head.

Thanks to all of my fellow outdoor writers who have helped me over the years. The late Paul Hope and Ed Holder were both instrumental in my career, and are greatly missed. Thanks also to Larry Bozka, David Sikes, Ron Henry Strait, Doug Pike, Shannon Tompkins, Joe Doggett, Gary Ralston, Nick Gilmore, Ted Venker, Luke Clayton, Greg Berlocher, and Robert Macias.

As anyone who has ever read my books knows, I get inspiration from all kinds of places, ranging from music to movies. Thanks to metal band Manowar for making the ultimate inspirational music, and to Iced Earth for giving me a template against which to judge my own music writing.

Thanks to George Lucas for creating the *Star Wars* universe, and for making "Episode 3" so awesome.

Thanks to Dr. Kent Hovind for his amazing research on the Bible and creation as it relates to science.

Also, thanks to my friends who have been there for me for many years. To Chris and Jamie Villadsen, Patrick and Amy Trumble, Lewis and Dominique Hogan, Todd and Valerie Sonnier, Shelly Johnston, Todd and Annie Jurasek, Jym and Beverly Evans, Reggie Salas, Ryan Warhola, Tommy Jerdee, and Clint Starling, know that I love you dearly.

To Frank Moore for being willing to venture out and do crazy things like chase wild boars around with dogs and knives, and to Jaclyn for raising some of the most wonderful children I have ever been around.

Thanks to all of my loyal supporters over the years who read my books, magazine and newspaper stories, and that listen to my radio program. You are truly amazing, and I want you to know your loyalty is greatly appreciated.

Finally, thanks to my dogs, Chyna, Sable, and the new pup (and hopefully great hunting retriever), Tarja. They make me smile every day, and sometimes we all need something in our lives to make that happen.

Index